COUNSELING AND PSYCHOTHERAPY SERVICES FOR UNIVERSITY STUDENTS

COUNSELING AND PSYCHOTHERAPY SERVICES FOR UNIVERSITY STUDENTS

Edited by

JOSEPH E. TALLEY, Ph.D.

Psychologist, Counseling and Psychological Services
Clinical Associate, Department of Psychiatry
Duke University
Durham, North Carolina

and

W. J. KENNETH ROCKWELL, M.D.

Assistant Professor, Department of Psychiatry
Psychiatrist, Counseling and Psychological Services
Duke University
Durham, North Carolina

With a Foreword by

Paul T. King, Ph.D.

President
American Board of
Professional Psychology

CHARLES C THOMAS • PUBLISHER
Springfield • Illinois • U.S.A.

Published and Distributed Throughout the World by

CHARLES C THOMAS • PUBLISHER

2600 South First Street

Springfield, Illinois 62717

© *1985 by* CHARLES C THOMAS • PUBLISHER

ISBN 0-398-05027-9

Library of Congress Catalog Card Number: 84-2526

With THOMAS BOOKS *careful attention is given to all details of manufacturing and design. It is the Publisher's desire to present books that are satisfactory as to their physical qualities and artistic possibilities and appropriate for their particular use.* THOMAS BOOKS *will be true to those laws of quality that assure a good name and good will.*

Printed in the United States of America
Q-R-3

Library of Congress Cataloging in Publication Data
Main entry under title:

Counseling and psychotherapy services for university
    students.

    Bibliography: p.
    Includes index.
    1. College students--Mental health services.
1. Talley, Joseph E.   II. Rockwell, W.J. Kenneth.
RC451.4.S7C68 1984   378'.19712   84-2526
ISBN 0-398-05027-9

CONTRIBUTORS

John C. Barrow, Ed.D., ABPP
Psychologist
Counseling and Psychological Services
Clinical Assistant Professor
Department of Psychiatry
Duke University
Durham, North Carolina

Christine D. Bell, M.S.W., ACSW
Clinical Social Worker
Counseling and Psychological Services
Clinical Instructor
Department of Psychiatry
Duke University
Durham, North Carolina

Karen H. Miller, M.D.
Former Student
Duke University Medical School
Durham, North Carolina
Currently, Resident in Internal Medicine
Tulane University Medical Center
New Orleans, Louisiana

Jane Clark Moorman, M.S.W., ACSW
Associate
Department of Psychiatry
Director and Clinical Social Worker
Counseling and Psychological Services
Duke University
Durham, North Carolina

W. J. Kenneth Rockwell, M.D.
Assistant Professor
Department of Psychiatry
Psychiatrist
Counseling and Psychological Services
Duke University
Durham, North Carolina

Donald R. Ross, M.D.
Former Chief Resident in Psychiatry
Duke University Medical Center
Durham, North Carolina
Currently, Staff Psychiatrist
The Sheppard and Enoch Pratt Hospital
Towson, Maryland

Elinor T. Roy, M.S.W., ACSW
Assistant Director and Clinical Social Worker
Counseling and Psychological Services
Clinical Associate
Department of Psychiatry
Duke University
Durham, North Carolina

Joseph E. Talley, Ph.D.
Psychologist
Counseling and Psychological Services
Clinical Associate
Department of Psychiatry

Duke University
Durham, North Carolina

John R. Urbach, M.D.
Former Chief Resident in Psychiatry
Duke University Medical Center
Durham, North Carolina
Currently, Staff Psychiatrist and Assistant Professor
Department of Psychiatry
New York Hospital-Westchester
Cornell Medical School
White Plains, New York

William W. K. Zung, M.D.
Professor
Department of Psychiatry
Duke University Medical Center
Durham, North Carolina

FOREWORD

IT is a distinct honor and pleasure to be asked to write the foreword for this fine and useful book. The book is divided into seven chapters of moderate length, each of which deals with an important dimension of the provision of psychological services in a university or college setting. The essential message of each chapter is clear and relatively compact. The various chapter authors stick to their topical headings, which gives the reader the pleasant task of reading relevant material, stripped of discursive writing, and presented in a lucid, easily comprehended style.

This book will have a strong appeal for those mental health practitioners who work with individuals struggling to master developmental problems in late adolescence and early adulthood. Consequently, health-service-provider psychologists, social workers, psychiatrists, psychiatric nurses, counselors, and clergymen should find something of value within these pages.

My immediate reaction to the book was an awareness of its far-reaching usefulness. I had a strong sense of tidiness about this manuscript, in that it brought together a discussion on many of the critical problem areas with which university-based psychological service centers are faced. The reader is conscious early in the book that the authors are addressing topics of concern, with which they have had vast experience, and about which they are able to write with a deep, reflective conversancy.

The special mission of the book is to clarify some of the service related aspects of the psychological/emotional problems presented by this age group, especially as represented by college and university students. The setting and experience background of the authors is clearly multidisciplinary. By this, I mean an integrated psychological service center that offers professional services in the areas of vocational counseling, career planning, psychosocial counseling, and both psychiatric treatment and consultation. Psychologists, both clinical and counseling, social workers, psychiatrists, and psychometricians are employed in this organization. The strong advantages for this multidisciplinary approach, as well as the philosophy behind it, are discussed in chapter three and several other places throughout the book.

The book is written in a clear, straight-forward manner even though ten different authors made contibutions. There is a uniformity in the way these authors approached main topics within the chapters that allows the transition from one chapter to another to be made without difficulty. I found this manner of approach to be an especially endearing aspect of this work, because much of the subject matter was obviously complex. The understanding by the reader was carefully kept in mind in the book's preparation.

The two opening chapters deal with comparisons of students who seek, and who do not seek, psychological services on college campuses. Chapter one addresses the demographic characteristics of students who seek help for broadly defined psychological problems at university-based counseling centers and mental health centers. The authors pull together important studies of the descriptors of students who seek help at college counseling centers. The literature review goes back a period of ten years. The content here is necessarily statistical in nature, but the information within will attract the attention of most student personnel workers in higher education. Although I have worked in University Counseling Centers for more than twenty-five years, I found much of this material to be new and enlightening, and other material to be confirmatory; I appreciated both effects.

The second chapter allows comparisons between students who have *not* sought professional assistance for their problems at university psychological services centers. Most of this chapter deals with a recent needs assessment survey of students attending Duke University, conducted by one of the authors of this book, and three other researchers. The author of the chapter compares the psychological needs of men versus women, of graduate and undergraduate students, of married and single students, and of non-minority and minority students. This chapter emphasizes the point that there "is a difference between what the general student body reports as important needs regarding counseling issues, and what those students who are sufficiently motivated to seek help (report) as needs." One conclusion that easily emerges from this chapter is that vocational and career counseling should be an integral part of a counseling center's professional service offerings. In a general sense, both experienced and budding professionals will gain from reading this book.

The counseling and/or mental health service administrator seeking to broaden the range of professional services at a campus agency gets a comprehensive exposition in the chapter concerned with the development of the multidisciplinary service at Duke University. The chapter would seem to have wide appeal in being translatable to other university settings whose campus administrators are consdering establishing multidisciplinary service agencies to meet their special particular campus situation. The rationale for agencies including several disciplines is cogently made. The author describes the merger process of the various service agencies and the professional disciplines that were ultimately integrated. It is an excellent example of the collaborative effort required by relevant university administrators who have the collective goal of improving student services, making them more accessible, as a pre-eminent purpose.

I found the chapters concerned with the in-take screening of depressed students, and consultation in psychiatric emergencies to include those issues which most staff members in psychological service agencies have the greatest need to know about, but often a lesser understanding. The authors make clear the incidence of depression among college students, as well as specific ways by which depressed students might be identified during the in-take process. The authors stress the importance of the early identification of depression in students, and the behavioral corollaries of depressed affect is pointed out in both the academic and psychosocial arenas.

When a student experiences a psychiatric emergency, it is an emotionally and physically stressful time for everyone concerned — counseling service and mental health professionals in several settings who must respond appropriately to the emergency, student personnel administrators, health service physicians, and most often, the student's parents. The issues that arise during these times are ones which must be handled sensitively. What are the ethical and legal issues involved? When is the notification of parents or relatives in emergencies truly appropriate? What university personnel should be consulted? Who does the notification of the parents? These "nervous" issues are explored in a reflective way which leaves the reader informed about matters which often he/she has not faced a great many times, and ones which rarely receive instructional attention in doctoral and/or intern training programs. This chapter deserves a "must read" designation for psychological interns as well as professional staff.

The chapter on the mental health professional's communication with parents of severely distressed students elaborates on many of the highly charged implications of imparting this sort of information to parents and relatives. The author shows a keen sensitivity to the ethical responsibility he has to the student, as well as demonstrating the importance of responding to the parents' anxiousness and understandable need for appropriate information about their son or daughter. The matter of hospitalizing the student, and how to bring the parents in on this process is explored. One of the main things to be learned from this chapter is how to deal with parents under a highly stressful situation while simultaneously attempting to enlist their continued support for the psychological intervention that probably lies ahead for their child. The author expertly informs the reader about maintaining that delicate balance of keeping the welfare of the student uppermost, while treating parents with empathy and respect.

The book is written in a down-to-earth expository manner. Its subject matter is well organized, and follows a logical progression which enhances its understandability.

To me, the book seems essential for workers in a large number of mental health settings, but especially for the college or university-based mental health professionals working in psychological service centers. A wide spectrum of relevant topics are discussed in a practical manner that will make them of immediate use to health service providers.

Paul T. King, Ph.D.
President
American Board of
Professional Psychology

PREFACE

A FIRST step in providing effective psychotherapy for any specific population is to understand as much as possible about the concerns and typical problems of that group. Moreover, learning about the context or environment in which treatment is offered gives a greater understanding of the situation in which treatment might best be delivered. The first chapter provides data concerning the presenting problems at several student mental health services and counseling centers and discusses various demographic factors associated with service usage. New data from a needs assessment study (Chapter II) show what concerns of a psychological or counseling nature are most prominent among students who do not seek psychological services. In this country most of these services on the college and university campus are provided through a counseling center or student mental health service and frequently two or more of such similar services exist on one campus. Chapter III describes the formation of an integrated multidisciplinary service at Duke University and discusses the way a consolidated service can effect the treatment of the student. The chapter is also of interest from an administrative perspective regarding the development of the service.

Other chapters addressing the administrative and mangement aspects of treatment focus on consultation with University administrators in psychiatric emergencies including the legal and ethical issues in such consultations, and what information should be released, to whom and when as well as a chapter on the often problematic issue of communications with parents. A chapter on the utilization of the Zung Self Rating Depression Scale as a regular part of the intake procedures with students presenting for psychotherapy or counseling of a psychosocial nature to assess the severity of depression has been included since suicide is an extremely significant treatment management issue in the late adolescent and young adult populations.

Finally, we have included a chapter on staff retreats from an organizational development perspective since the purpose of such retreats is toward the enhancement of staff morale as well as solving problems facing the agency. Thus, staff retreats can affect the psychotherapeutic treatment of students in several indirect ways.

The aim of this book is to provide new information and discussion regarding the administrative, contextual and management aspects of counseling and psychotherapy with university students.

We would like to clarify how some terms in the text are used. First, the words "client," "patient," and "student" are used somewhat interchangeably. The context determined which term seemed most appropriate. Second, the terms "treatment," "psychotherapy," "therapy," and "counseling" (when not specified as some type other than psychosocial) are all used to mean individual psychotherapeutic treatment of some type. Again, the selection of the term was made on the basis of what appeared most appropriate given the context. Occasionally the term "personal counseling" may appear. We have for the most part eschewed this term in favor of "psychosocial counseling" since all individual counseling is personal whatever the topic. Finally, every effort has been made to avoid the generic use of the masculine and feminine pronouns and in most cases this has been possible without a loss of clarity. However, in many instances we have used both the masculine and feminine pronouns despite the slight sacrifice to awkwardness and occasionally generic use provided the only readable alternative.

ACKNOWLEDGMENTS

WE would like to express our appreciation to Mrs. Helen T. Biggers for superbly performing the difficult task of coordinating all of our data collection and to Mrs. Alyce B. Williams for her faithful assistance in this. Our thanks go to Mrs. Sharon M. Jacobs for her excellent secretarial work throughout the preparation process and for her typing of the final copy of our manuscript. We are indebted to Ms. Jean C. Hughes for her invaluable editorial assistance.

Many faculty and administrators have played crucial roles in the development and continued support of Counseling and Psychological Services at Duke University. Their efforts have enabled us to engage in some research related to our work with students. Although naming each individual would be impossible, we have especially benefitted from the close involvement of Drs. H. Keith H. Brodie, Robert C. Carson, and Robert N. Sawyer. Former Provost Frederic N. Cleaveland gave tirelessly to the formation and early development of our Service and William J. Griffith, Vice President of Student Affairs, has encouraged our pursuits in all areas with a personal interest.

Finally do the editors salute their wives, Vibeke and Meta, incomparable unseen companions to this project.

J.E.T.
W.J.K.R.

CONTENTS

COUNSELING AND PSYCHOTHERAPY SERVICES FOR UNIVERSITY STUDENTS

Chapter I.

WHO SEEKS PSYCHOLOGICAL SERVICES ON CAMPUS AND WHY?

W. J. KENNETH ROCKWELL AND JOSEPH E. TALLEY

TO anyone engaged in planning and delivering psychological services for students in the system of higher education, the questions posed in this chapter's title are important. The information to be presented that responds to these questions is useful, but it must be put into the perspective that it is derived from a limited number of studies on selected populations of students. As to the large scene, there are approximately 3,200 colleges, universities, and branch campuses in the United States at this time.[1] No comprehensive survey exists of counseling and mental health services available to or through the schools, and it is safe to say that the majority of them do not have a discrete Service identified as an administrative entity. Thus, a large but unknown percentage of the 11 to 12 million students enrolled in institutions of higher education in this country do not seek formal psychological services on campus simply because they are not available. This does not mean that none of these students seek out and receive similar or other services off campus. Like-

---

[1]Figures given for characteristics of the U. S. population engaged in higher education are derived from *Digest of Education Statistics,* 1982, National Center for Education Statistics, W. Vance Grant and Leo J. Eidens, Superintendent of Documents, U. S. Government Printing Office, Washington, D.C. 20402.

wise, a substantial percentage of students use non-university affiliated counseling and psychological services even when a Center is made available by their school. One can find in the literature no substantial basis for comparing those who come to a university-based Service and that large percentage of students who seek professional services elsewhere.

The words "college student" still conjure up the image of someone between the ages of eighteen and twenty-two going a progress through eight consecutive semesters, probably among ivy. Although this stereotype may be fading, the literature on normal development and psychopathology in the college population predominantly reflects study of the undergraduate. Whereas approximately 75 percent of college students are undergraduates, more than one-third of all college students are part-time and more than 12 percent are thirty-five years of age and over. Further breakdown of the various demographic characteristics of college students reveals that they are an extremely heterogeneous lot, and becoming more so.

The answers to the question "Who Comes To The College Psychological Services Center and Why?" are based on studies done in well established campus-based centers and slanted toward the undergraduate. Many more studies are required in order to get a comprehensive picture of the need for services in the total population engaged in higher education.

In order to understand the utilization of psychological services on those campuses where they exist, it is first necessary to put that utilization in context with respect to the types of agencies. Many if not most campuses have a model whereby a student mental health service and a counseling center exist separately. The student mental health service is usually staffed by psychiatrists, psychiatric residents, clinical social workers, and psychiatric nurses, while the counseling center is most often staffed by psychologists. The counseling center usually does educational, vocational, and marital counseling as well as psychotherapy, whereas the mental health service may be more involved in emergency situations requiring medication and hospitalization as well as psychotherapy. Thus, there is often a significant overlap with regard to the activity known as psychotherapy.

It may appear from this description that a mental health service would serve more severely disturbed students with greater psychopathology than would a counseling center. A study at Michigan State University (Aniskiewicz, 1979) investigated this supposed difference between the clienteles of the two services there and found that no statistically significant differences existed between those students who used the counseling center and those who used the mental health service regarding the level of the distress associated with the presenting concern when the problem was not primarily vocational or educational in nature. Aniskiewicz suggests that the findings support the contention that the utilization patterns of a counseling center will depend on the emphasis given to its psychotherapy as opposed to its vocational/educational activity.

In evaluating reports of utilization patterns, it is essential to be aware of the particular idiosyncrasies of any agencies as well as the campus environment surrounding them, including the nature of the student body. For example, data reported from studies at the University of Cincinnati must be viewed in the context of the school as a large urban university in which a mental health program was established to do primarily crisis intervention and emergency work. The University of Cincinnati might also be described as a "commuter school" and has a higher percentage of older and married students than many other universities. Further, although the University of Cincinnati's service has a multidisciplinary staff, they do not offer vocational, educational, or marital counseling. In contrast, despite the fact that Duke's service is also mutlidisciplinary, the population seen is understandably different since the Duke service is designed to provide vocational, educational, and marital counseling in addition to other services. Thus, when comparing data reported from Duke and from Cincinnati it must be remembered that each agency is in all likelihood perceived somewhat differently by the students at least in part due to the fact that the services offered are not identical. In short, utilization will obviously be affected by the services offered. It must also be remembered that Duke is a private university of moderate size in the Southeast that attracts for the most part preprofessional students and that the majority of undergraduates are between the ages of eighteen and twenty-two. The University of Cincinnati is quite different from this in terms of location, size, and the composition of the student body.

Further, it is important to be cognizant of the fact that presenting problems do not necessarily indicate the most frequently occurring psychological problems found in the campus community as a whole. A study done at Washington University (Rimmer, Halikas, and Schuckit, 1982) revealed that over a four year period 39 percent of their selected sample of students experienced a "psychiatric illness" but that only about one quarter of those students sought any form of treatment. However, in this study if a student from the sample sought assistance for academic problems such as study skills or for career counseling at the counseling center s/he was not counted as having sought treatment. This raises the possibility that students having an emotional disturbance may have sought help for a concern felt to be less threatening, even though there was a more pervasive problem causing the presenting concern. Moreover, only one-third of all students who did seek some form of psychological treatment at the mental health clinic had a diagnosable psychiatric problem. Thus, this study underscores three important issues in counseling in campus psychological services: (1) many students with psychological problems will not seek any assistance; (2) many students seeking psychological services do not have a psychiatric diagnosis; and (3) students with a serious psychological problem may ask for help with a less serious problem.

DEMOGRAPHIC FACTORS

Age

A study done at Washington University (Rimmer, Halikas, and Schuckit, 1982) found that of those students developing a psychiatric problem 18 percent occurred during the first year of college, 14 percent in the second and again in the third year of college, and 19 percent in the fourth year. It would appear from these data that the senior year is the time of greatest psychological vulnerability. Further corroboration is given by Selig and Weiss (1975) at the University of Cincinnati who found seniors most likely to use the mental health service and freshmen least likely to use it. In marked contrast Sharp and Kirk (1974) found that the rate of students initiating contact for counseling services declined "steeply over time both by years and by quarters within years." It is noteworthy that the University of Cincinnati study was conducted at a mental health center, while the Sharp and Kirk study was conducted at the University of California at Berkeley's Counseling Center. The differences in the types of services may have influenced results. Support for this idea is found in our 1982-83 data from Duke which show a mean age of 19.9 years for students coming with vocational and educational concerns and 21.4 years for those presenting with psychosocial problems. Finally Wogan and Amdur (1974) at the University of Connecticut concluded that students in their patient population did not vary significantly in age from those in the general student population; however, an increase from 19.8 to 20.8 as the mean age of their clinic population did occur from 1964 to 1972. At the Duke Service for the year 1981-1982 the most frequently presenting single age was nineteen with eighteen and twenty years olds being roughly equal as second categories while twenty-one year olds (mostly seniors) were seen least frequently. An important finding regarding age from the Duke data is that the percentage of seventeen year old freshmen coming for service was three times that of those freshmen who were eighteen years old or older. Furthermore, a disproportionate number of the seventeen year olds received medication or were hospitalized. Therefore if age alone is considered, our data indicate a decreasing likelihood of seeking services as the student ages. However, the results reported from different schools are conflicting and consequently the role of other mitigating variables must be considered.

Time and Timing Factors

Seasonal variation and rate of presentation is an interesting phenomenon. Sharp and Kirk (1974) found fall to be the time of the year for most intakes. This finding is supported by our data at Duke showing September and October to be the months with the greatest number of initial contacts. However, Selig and Weiss (1975) found that the winter months were most likely to show more new presentations at the University of Cincinnati. At Duke, March and April have proven to be the busier months in terms of total number of students coming to the Service.

The percentage of transfer students seeking psychological services at Duke is much higher than the non-transfer population and most transfer students are nineteen or twenty years of age. Wogan and Amdur (1974) at the University of Connecticut and Downey and Sinnett (1980) at Kansas State University also reported a high percentage of transfer students in their clinic populations. The differences found at Connecticut were statistically significant in that 38 percent of the clinic population were transfer students while only 14 percent of the general population were transfer students. It is interesting to note that all of the twenty-one transfer students presenting to our Service in the 1982-1983 school year sought help with psychosocial problems and none with vocational or educational problems.

Former students returning to school also show a higher percentage of presentation for psychosocial services. For example, during the 1982-83 Duke academic year, only two of thirty-five, or 6 percent, of such students coming to Counseling and Psychological Services sought vocational/educational help. These groups identified as having higher presenting percentage rates than the remainder of the population are more apart from the mainstream of college life, at least initially, due to their differences in student status. Therefore, it may be that students who are, or feel that they are, in some way cut off from the majority of students become more vulnerable to psychological problems.

Place of Residence

Duke students who live off-campus or in campus housing that is more remote from the main campus are more likely to request psychological services than those who live on-campus. Although the University of Cincinnati study by Selig and Weiss (1975) reported a higher percentage of psychological services use by on-campus students, the authors emphasized that the University of Cincinnati was a commuter school with more than 85 percent of the student body living off-campus. These off-campus students were reported to be more often older and married whereas the percentage of the Duke off-campus population was much smaller and the majority of these students were not married. Since these student bodies are so divergent it is understandable that a very different type of student would feel apart from the mainstream at each school. Additionally, Selig and Weiss noted that those persons living off-campus were more likely to be married, and they speculated that the married students' spouses were a source of support. The findings of Wogan and Amdur (1974) at the University of Connecticut were similar to the findings at Duke in that the clinic sample they examined in 1972 was more likely to have students living off-campus than would be expected and this difference was statistically significant. However, in their 1964 data Wogan and Amdur found that on-campus students presented for psychological services at a disproportionate rate to their occurrence in the population. Obviously these results did not seem to fit together with great ease, but it is possible that living on-campus in the mid-1960's was more stressful than living off-campus, whereas subsequently the opposite may have been true.

The on-campus vs. off-campus factor as it relates to utilization may be heavily influenced by the physical prominence of the psychological service on the campus and by the length of time the service has been in existence. An agency that has high physical visibility but is relatively new might be more utilized by on-campus students simply due to its ease of access, whereas a service that has been in existence for quite some time and enjoys a position of familiarity with the student body as a whole may be more utilized by off-campus students.

Sex

Most demographic studies address the issue of sex, and the literature appears consistent enough to draw the conclusion that women present for service more frequently than men. Wogan and Amdur (1974) noted that presenting students were more likely to be females in 1972 than they were in 1964 despite the fact that there were more women than men presenting in 1964; however, the difference was statistically significant in 1972 only, when 57 percent of the clinic sample were women while women comprised just 42 percent of the university enrollment. In the University of Cincinnati study (Selig and Weiss, 1975) a disporportionate number of women were found coming to the agency (55 percent) compared with their representa-

the student body (40 percent).

An investigation surveying New England college undergraduates (Wechsler, Roman, and Soloman, 1981) attempted to find out what percentage of students experienced certain emotional and psychological difficulties. The authors found that women reported more problems than men and particularly that women reported more difficulty with weight control and with making decisions than did men. Rimmer, Halikas, and Schuckit (1982) also found a higher incidence of psychological difficulty among women than men at Washington University but the difference was not statistically significant. At Duke 60 percent of students coming to the Service in 1981-1982 were women and 40 percent were men while the university population was comprised of 59 percent men and 41 percent women. The literature is consistent in finding that women seek psychological services more frequently than men do. The reason for this is open to speculation. The data have important implications for outreach education and small group experiences on certain themes of interest to women.

Marital Status

Since it is difficult to assess the percentage of married students in the general student population, figures can rarely be examined in a reliable manner that compare married students with single students regarding the utilization of psychological services. Nevertheless, in the Kansas State study (1980) Downey and Sinett conclude that their presenting students were more likely to be married than single whereas at the University of Connecticut Wogan and Amdur (1974) reported that only 16 percent of the students seen were married. The conclusion of Wogan and Amdur that the rates of emotional disturbance are as high among married students as single students seems acceptable given the very limited data comparing the marital status of presenting students to the marital status of the general student population.

Area of Study

Another factor that appears to be related to the utilization of psychological services is major area of study. The 1981-82 data from Duke indicated that nursing students and students majoring in the humanities or social sciences were more likely to seek psychological services than those students majoring in the natural sciences, mathematics, or engineering at the undergraduate level. The percentage of students seen for services in the entire university population was 11.5. At the graduate and professional school level the following percentages of enrolled students were seen: Divinity School, 11; Graduate School of Arts and Sciencs, 7.5; Medical School, 6.4; Law School, 6; and Business School, only 3.3 despite the fact that at that time the Business School was in the same building as Counseling and Psychological Services. These findings at Duke corroborated those of Scheff (1966) who found that students from the social and behavioral sciences as well as from the humanities were overrepresented as users of psychological services while the natural sciences and professional schools were underrepresented. Selig and Weiss (1975) found that usage was high among students from the schools of arts and sciences, and business administration. Selig and Weiss acknowledged that to some extent geographic proximity might have affected usage but they speculated that students in the health fields and in areas of study encouraging (overt) self expression valued psychotherapy highly, at least in part due to their being at home in verbal self-expression.

TYPE OF SERVICE SOUGHT

Type of Problem/Concern

With respect to the concerns of students presenting themselves to psychological services on campus, the data from Duke's Counseling and Psychological Services in 1981-82 are probably fairly representative and are presented in Table I. Students most frequently reported their problems as interpersonal with the symptomatic affect being depression or anxiety. The next most frequent reasons for presentation were vocational or educational problems often accompanied by the same affects but usually less intense. Alcohol and drug problems as well as phobias presented least frequently as the primary concern.

Table I

PRIMARY PRESENTING PROBLEM

a). **Content**		b). **Associated Affect**	
1. Intrapersonal	252	Anxiety/fear/panic/tension	352
2. Family	72	Depression	267
3. Marital	79	Grief reaction	20
4. Other interpersonal	74	Suicidal feelings	7
5. Sexual	23	Anger/hostility	51
6. Problem pregnancy	7	Loss of feeling/apathy	41
7. Obsessional	28	Other or none	301
8. Phobic	8	Total	1,039
9. Alienation/isolation	27		
10. Drugs/alcohol	2		
11. Thought disorder	4		
12. Suspiciousness	5		
13:.Concern about another	0		
14. Vocational/Educational	339		
15. Other	119		
Total	1,039		

Parental Divorce and Death

Fewer than 15 percent of Duke students in 1981-82 responding to the question on the intake form had parents who were separated or divorced. This would appear to be a relatively low percentage rate. To the clinician who listens to the emotional distress of students whose parents are going through a divorce it may seem difficult to believe that this percentage is in all likelihood less than the percentage of the general student population with divorced parents. Approximately 8 percent of students seeking services had a deceased parent, but the percentage of all students at the University having a deceased parent was not known. The literature, clinical experience, and common experience indicate that such a significant loss has profound effects but further studies need to be done to detemine if students with deceased parents have indeed greater risk for psychological problems and if this is so, what interventions if any might be applied to reduce the risk.

Diagnosis

A four year prospective study done at Washington University (Rimmer, Halikas, and Schuckit, 1982) revealed that 90 percent of those students assessed to have psychiatric difficulty as defined by the *Diagnositc and Statistical Manual Of Mental Disorders III* (DSM III) were depressed. These authors suggest that the common diagnoses of identity disorder and adjustment disorder may in many cases be more appropriately diagnosed as depression. The Duke findings concerning affect on presentation were similar to the findings of Wogan and Amdur (1974) who noted affective difficulties (i.e., depression, anxiety) as the most frequently occurring presenting complaints by students. Hersch, Nazario, and Backus (1983) at the University of Massachusetts with a sample of two hundred university students found the most prevalent Axis I diagnoses to be as follows: phase of life problem or other life circumstance problem (N=72), adjustment disorder with depressed mood (N=28), adjustment disorder with mixed emotional features (N=26), other interpersonal problem (N=12), dysthymic disorder (N=9), generalized anxiety disorder (N=5), major depression (N=4), ego dystonic homosexuality (N=3) and cannabis dependence (N=2). In terms of DSM-III diagnostic criteria the Duke 1981-82 data appear as follows in Table II.

Table II

DIAGNOSTIC DATA

AXIS I Diagnosis		AXIS II Diagnosis	
No diagnosis	35%	No diagnosis	83%
Phase of life or life circumstance problem	13%	Diagnosis deferred	9%
		Borderline personality	1%
Academic problem	4¹/₂%	Histrionic personality	1%
Occupational (choice) problem	3¹/₂%	Passive-dependent personality	1¹/₂%
Other interpersonal problem	2%	Obsessive-compulsive personality	1¹/₂%
Marital problem	2%		
Eating disorder	2¹/₂%		

Table II (continued)

AXIS I Diagnosis		AXIS II Diagnosis
Dysthymic disorder	3%	
Bipolar affective disorder	1%	
Psychosis or thought process disorder	3¹/₂%	
Adjustment disorder with depressed mood	6%	
Adjustmen disorder with anxious mood	3¹/₂%	
Adjustment disorder with mixed emotional features	1%	
Identity disorder`	1%	
Diagnosis deferred	11%	

All other diagnoses occurred at a frequency of less than 1 percent.

This detail is given in order to make it apparent that while there may be a wide variety of psychological problems presented to a campus center if it offers a broad range of services, there are nevertheless certain diagnostic categories that represent the types of students currently likely to seek psychological services. When considering the data presented from our service it is of course necessary to look at other data (see Needs Assessment chapter) in order to maintain a more comprehensive perspective as to what troubles college students the most, including those not seeking help.

SUMMARY AND CONCLUSIONS

Several studies have addressed the questions of who seeks psychological services on campus and why, and although the number and scope of the studies are limited relative to the size and diversity of the total college population, the findings are probably quite representative insofar as demographic factors are concerned. When age has been investigated conflicting findings have emerged. Studies done at student mental health services have for the most part foundthe likelihood of presentation to increase over the college years while studies conducted at counseling centers have reported the opposite and data from our combined service indicate no significant difference between age groups concerning the probability of presenting for help. However, we do find that younger students present more often for vocational or educational services than older students who present more often with psychosocial concerns. Thus, it seems that the type of services an agency offers is most influential in determining the ages of students seeking help there. Women have consistently presented themselves for help at agencies of all types in greater percentages than men, whereas there have been no consistent findings with respect to marital status. Likewise, the findings have been mixed with regard to living on *vs.* living off campus, but a trend in the data suggests that a greater proportion of off-campus than on-campus students have been seeking psychological services in recent years. In looking at field of study, students most likely to present for psychological services are apt to be from groups stereotypically thought to be more verbally or artistically expressive and more accepting of the use of such services. Students from fields such as the physical sciences, technical schools, and engineering have been consistently reported to seek services less frequently. In regard to student status, at least two of the studies discussed have found transfer students to present more frequently than the general student population. Other data reported suggested that freshmen beginning in January, former students returning to school, and seventeen year old freshmen are seen with greater frequency than would be expected.

Data that deal with types of problems and diagnoses are less numerous and less neat than demographic data, and it is more difficult to comprehend their meaning. Students who seek help are likely to be anxious and/or depressed symptomatically, regardless of other considerations. Beyond that, whether the presenting problem is labeled as "vocational/educational" or "normal developmental" or as a "diagnosis," all are personal problems and as such are related to the host of internal non-status variables that tend to confound attempts at explanation anyway. With respect to formal psychiatric diagnosis, all diagnostic entities will be found represented in the higher education population except moderate degrees of mental retardation and chronic organic brain syndrome, and those diagnoses assigned only to children. There are too few data comparing symptomatic states, problem types, and diagnoses of those students who seek services and those who do not to make generalizations.

The data derived so far support two hypotheses, among others, and not astonishingly both hypotheses relate to what is called the process of adjustment. The first hypothesis is that students who feel like misfits in the campus environment, whatever that environment is, are more likely to seek psychological services than those who do not feel like misfits.

There are probably few student demographic or diagnostic variables *per se* that differentiate help seekers and non-seekers, but a student's perception of the relationship of those variables to the school environment strongly influences her/his sense of well-being.

The second hypothesis is that students who are in a transitional status are more likely to seek help than those who are not. Transfer students, first year graduate or professional students, and perhaps freshmen and seniors are such people, and for them the problem is how to adjust.

Factors influencing students to seek help must always be viewed in the context of the university environment, since it is more often the fit between student and environment rather than individual factors that determine the student's sense of well-being.

REFERENCES

1. Aniskiewicz, A. S.: Symptom characteristics of counseling center and mental health service clients. *Journal of Counseling Psychology, 26*(4):355-358, 1979.
2. Downey, R., and Sinnett, E.: Characteristics of students seeking mental health services. *Journal of College Student Personnel, 21*(1):9-14, 1980.
3. Hersch, J., Nazario, N., and Backus, B.: DSM III and the college mental health setting: The University of Massachusetts experience. *Journal of American College Health, 31*(6):247-252, 1983.
4. Rimmer, H. J., Halikas, G. A., and Schuckit, M.: Prevalence and incidence of psychiatric illness in college students: a four year prospective study. *Journal of American College Health, 30*(5):207-211, 1982.
5. Scheff, T. J.: Users and non-users of a student psychiatric clinic. *Journal of Health and Human Behavior, 7*(2):114-121, 1966
6. Selig, S. and Weiss, S.: Non-psychological factors affecting the utilization of a mental health facility. *Journal of the American College Health Association, 23*(4):299-303, 1975.
7. Sharp, W., and Kirk, B.: Counseling when. *Journal of Counseling*

Psychology, 2(1):43-50, 1974.

8. Wechsler, H., Rohman, M., Solomon, L.: Some correlates of emotional well-being among New England college students. *Journal of the American College Health Association,* 29(5):221-223, 1981.

9. Wogan, M., and Amdur, M.: Changing patterns of student mental health. *Journal of the American College Health Association,* 22(3):202-208, 1974.

Chapter II.

PSYCHOLOGICAL NEEDS REPORTED BY STUDENTS NOT SEEKING SERVICES

JOSEPH E. TALLEY

I N order to understand the psychological needs of the university population more completely, the needs of students who do not seek help must be considered as well as the needs expressed by those who do. One means of doing this is to conduct a needs assessment survey.

Carney and Barak (1976) conducted a survey of seniors at Ohio State University to determine student service-related needs in general and found that choice of major and choice of career were the primary concerns expressed. The priorities of university mental health needs as identified by students have been compared to those identified by professionals (Henggeler, Sallis and Cooper, 1980) and "extensive" differences were found. Career choice was rated as the number one need among twenty-four options by the professionals and as eighth by students, who rated alcohol and drug problems as most important.

Weissberg, Berentsen, Cote, Cravey and Heath (1982), however, found that students expressed stronger needs in the career development area than in academic or personal areas. Alcohol and drug-related problems were rated as not very important by these students. It was also found that female students expressed more concern than males with regard to dealing with personal conflicts, expressing opinions and thoughts directly, controlling weight and developing independence. Males expressed stronger needs on understanding more about love and intimacy. Students as a whole expressed low needs concerning homesickness, alcohol and drugs, parents' divorce, relationship with parents and birth control. Kramer, Berger and Miller (1974) at Cornell University also found students to be most concerned with vocational identity and least concerned with drugs and abortion. These authors found a similarity of concerns across sex and class.

An investigation focusing on married students conducted by Flores (1978), concluded that married students sense different needs than unmarried students. Indrisano and Auerbach (1979) have compared the needs of students applying for mental health services to those who did not. Students not seeking help ranked vocational and study concerns as a much higher priority than those students who did seek services. A needs assessment survey conducted at Duke University (Talley, Barrow, Fulkerson, and Moore, 1983) utilized a fifty-two item questionnaire (see Appendix I) listing a number of needs that would appear to be important to the college student based in part on previous questionnaires (Henggeler, Sallis and Cooper, 1980; Rue and Lawler, 1980). The student was asked to rate the current importance of each need on a scale of one to five with one being "not important" and five being "extremely important." Although the questionnaire was completed anonymously some demographic data were requested. The student was also asked to indicate a preference for mode of service delivery for each item (i.e., a one-to-one format, a small group or an educational presentation). The subjects were 269 students who returned the questionnaire by mail and eighty-four students contacted by telephone. The mean age of the total sample was 21.44 years. Originally, the questionnaire was mailed to 779 students and telephone contact was attempted with 106 students. Of those responding, 188 were males (mean age, 21.33) 158 were females (mean age, 20.75) and seven did not identify their sex. The sample was selectively drawn from the Registrar's file such that every tenth full-time student was in the group. Many of the students had moved or left school, thus making contact impossible. It was discovered that the priorities of students interviewed by telephone were almost identical to those contacted by mail. The findings are also quite interesting due to the fact that vocational planning related items were rated as of most importance. The data were analyzed to see if differences in the ratings of needs existed between graduate/ professional *vs.* undergraduate students, male *vs.* female students, male graduate/professional *vs.* female graduate/professional students, married students, and minority students.

In deference to methodological accuracy, it must be noted that minority and married students are compared to the general sample and not to non-minority and single students. However, since these two subgroups had such a small N compared to the total sample, the comparisons should still be meaningful.

NEEDS ASSESSMENT RESULTS

In comparing the needs expressed by women and men, it is interesting that the top six items were identical although there was some slight variation in rank order based on means after the first two items, "Planning my career or vocation" and "Understanding my interests, skills, values, and personality," a career related task. Table I shows the order of those items along with their relative rankings by sex.

Table I

NEEDS ASSESSMENT

MEAN RATING BY ALL MEN
(N = 188, MEAN AGE = 22.13)
OF SOME IMPORTANCE (3) OR MORE

		Rating
1.	Planning my career or vocation	3.54
2.	Understanding my interests, skills, abilities and personality	3.38
3.	Communicating more effectively	3.11
4.	Coping with the stresses in my life	3.09
5.	Finding written information about careers and educational programs	3.08
6.	Setting reasonable expectations for myself	3.05
7.	Making decisions and solving problems	3.04
8.	Enriching a relationship I have	3.03

MEAN RATING BY ALL WOMEN
(N = 159, MEAN AGE = 20.75)
OF SOME IMPORTANCE (3) OR MORE

		Rating
1.	Planning my career or vocation	3.74
2.	Understanding my interests, skills, values and personality	3.62
3.	Coping with stresses in my life	3.56
4.	Setting reasonable expectations for myself	3.53
5.	Communicating more effectively	3.36
6.	Finding written information about careers and educational programs	3.29
7.	Developing self-confidence and self-esteem	3.28
8.	Making decisions and solving problems	3.24
9.	Assertively standing up for myself	3.22
10.	Enriching a relationship I have	3.20
11.	Lessening procrastination	3.13
12.	Managing my time effectively	3.12
13.	Improving my relationships with others	3.11
14.	Developing my helping skills (listening, communicating, caring, etc.)	3.06
15.	Finding and enjoying leisure time	3.00

Another interesting feature of these data is the number of items rated as of "some importance" (three) or more by each group. Men found only eight items to be at least of some importance while women rated fifteen items to be of at least some importance. This is especially relevant in light of the fact that more women actually do present for services than men. It is also apparent that the women in the sample tended to rate most items higher than the men did. This was particularly true for a number of items relating to assertiveness, self-esteen, making friends and making decisions. The women may have been more honest about their feelings, or they may have more concerns about their personal "selves" than do the men of this population.

Concerning the graduate/professional students, the men rated only four items as of at least some importance and again these were the career-related items (see Table II), as well as the item about enriching a relationship. The ratings of most items by the graduate men were lower than the ratings by the total male sample.

Graduate/professional women rated twelve items to be of at least some importance and those rated as more important were psychosocial rather than vocational in content. Yet most of these items were also rated highly by the total sample of women. It is apparent that overall ratings were lower for graduate women than the total sample of women, analogous to the findings for graduate men, although the difference was not as profound with the women.

Table II

NEEDS ASSESSMENT

MEAN RATINGS BY MALE GRADUATE STUDENTS
(N = 71, MEAN AGE = 26.70)
OF SOME IMPORTANCE (3) OR MORE

	Rating
1. Planning my career or vocation	3.12
2. Enriching a relationship I have	3.05
3. Understanding my interests, skills, values and personality	3.01
4. Being part of a two career couple	3.00

MEAN RATINGS BY FEMALE GRADUATE STUDENTS
(N = 45, MEAN AGE = 23.58)
OF SOME IMPORTANCE (3) OR MORE

	Rating
1. Being part of a two career couple	3.62
2. Coping with the stresses in my life	3.53
3. Communicating more effectively	3.40
4. Setting reasonable expectations for myself	3.23
5. Understanding my interests, skills, values and personality	3.20
6. Making decisions and solving problems	3.18
7. Planning my career or vocation	3.13
8. Developing self-confidence and self-esteem	3.12
9. Managing my time effectively	3.11
10. Assertively standing up for myself	3.09
11. Combining family, school and career	3.09
12. Developing my leadership skills	3.07
13. Exploring my marital expectations	3.05

In contrasting the group of minority students to the total sample, item four regarding career and vocational planning was the highest for the minority gorup as it was for the total sample. The other items rated as of some importance or more by minority students (see Table III) were rated similarly by at least one of the other sample sub-groups discussed, with the exception of the item on dealing with homesickness. This raises the question of whether minority students experience a greater sense of displacement in leaving their home and neighborhoods than other students do. On the whole, however, the minority group in this study did not differ substantially from the rest of the sample in terms of reported needs. Nevertheless, before concluding that no special services should be provided for the minority population it must be acknowledged that this particular minority sample may differ significantly from samples at other universities. Moreover, this group was between one third and one half Asian (some students did not indicate their specific background).

Table III

NEEDS ASSESSMENT

MEAN RATINGS BY MINORITY STUDENTS
(N = 28, MEAN AGE = 19.73)
OF SOME IMPORTANCE (3) OR MORE

	Rating
1. Planning my career or vocation	3.61
2. Coping with the stresses in my life	3.46
3. Communicating more effectively	3.43
4. Developing my leadership skills	3.27
5. Improving my relationships with others	3.27
6. Making decisions and solving problems	3.25
7. Managing my time effectively	3.25
8. Assertively standing up for myself	3.11
9. Understanding my interests, skills, values and personality	3.07
10. Getting myself energized to tackle my goals	3.04
11. Being part of a two career couple	3.00

As a subgroup, married students rated the fewest number of

needs, only four, as of some importance (see Table IV), and they were centered around issues relating to marriage such as the item on combining family, school, and work, the item on being part of a two career couple and the time management item.

Table IV

NEEDS ASSESSMENT

MEAN RATINGS BY MARRIED STUDENTS
(N = 27, MEAN AGE = 30.44)
OF SOME IMPORTANCE (3) OR MORE

	Rating
1. Combining family and school/career	3.38
2. Being part of a two career couple	3.33
3. Managing my time effectively	3.15
4. Enriching a relationship I have	3.00

As is evident from Table V, undergraduates on the whole rated most items as more important than graduate/professional students did. The undergraduates also rated more items as of at least some importance. The principal difference is the primacy of a marital issue for the graduate/professional students, and this is in all likelihood largely due to the age difference.

Table V

NEEDS ASSESSMENT

MEAN RATINGS BY ALL UNDERGRADUATES
(N = 231, MEAN AGE = 19.40)
OF SOME IMPORTANCE (3) OR MORE

	Rating
1. Planning my career or vocation	3.87
2. Understanding my interests, skills, values and personality	3.68
3. Finding information about careers and educational programs	3.45

4.	Coping with the stresses in my life	3.38
5.	Setting reasonable expectations for myself	3.35
6.	Communicating more effectively	3.32
7.	Making decisions and solving problems	3.22
8.	Improving my relationships with others	3.20
9.	Enriching a relationship I have	3.20
10.	Getting myself energized to tackle my goals	3.19
11.	Lessening procrastination	3.12
12.	Developing my helping skills (listening, communicating, caring, etc.)	3.12
13.	Managing my time effectively	3.10
14.	Assertively standing up for myself	3.09
15.	Developing self-confidence and self-esteem	3.07

MEAN RATINGS BY ALL GRADUATE/PROFESSIONAL STUDENTS
(N = 116, MEAN AGE = 25.49)
OF SOME IMPORTANCE (3) OR MORE

		Rating
1.	Being part of a two career couple	3.25
2.	Coping with the stresses in my life	3.17
3.	Planning my career or vocation	3.13
4.	Understanding my interests, skills, values and personality	3.09
5.	Setting reasonable expectations for myself	3.07
6.	Communicating more effectively	3.04
7.	Managing my time effectively	3.00

DISCUSSION

In looking at the results across groups, age is obviously an intervening variable and considerably affects comparisons between subgroups. For example, married students have the highest mean age, minority students have the lowest mean age. The number of needs rated as of some importance or more decreases as the mean age of the group increases. Age itself may be the most significant factor. Further, these data suggest when viewed as a whole that the younger female minority undergraduate student who is single had the greatest likelihood of experiencing at least one of these items as of some importance at the time surveyed, and that older married male graduate students of Caucasian background were the least likely to experience (or report) one of these items as of some importance at the time surveyed.

In contrasting the needs of those who present for services *vs.* the needs rated as most important by a random sample of students it is imperative to bear in mind that none of the items on the question-narie had a mean rating of four ("quite important") or more. Hope-fully, most students do not experience an intense need with regard to items indicating psychological difficulty. In fact, it would be surpris-ing if a mean of four or more did occur. Of course, students who do experience an item as important may indeed not experience it as im-portant enough to motivate them to seek help with the concern. The type of items listed on this questionnaire are mostly situational and perhaps more relevant to the services of a counseling center than to a student mental health service and most of the items were possible to endorse without presenting as socially undesirable. Nevertheless, all items except 16, 22 and 47 were rated as "extremely important" by at least 10 percent of the sample.

In comparing the survey data to data regarding presenting prob-lem on intake, four-fifths of the students presenting to the Duke Ser-vice for individual work in 1981-82 came with a psychosocial rather than a vocational or educational problem, whereas the general stu-dent population found the latter issues more problematic. Although the questionnaire did not address such problems as severe depres-sion or acute anxiety attacks, the results do emphasize that there is a difference between what the general student body reports as impor-tant needs regarding counseling issues and what those students who are sufficiently motivated to seek help present with as needs.

One important difference in the methodology of needs assess-ment surveys is how the students are asked what is important to them. Our study at Duke and others cited earlier which found low ratings for drug and alcohol problems but high ratings on vocational choice items specifically asked students to indicate problems that they had personally felt important recently. Studies finding high rat-ings on drugs and alcohol as problem areas asked students to report what they thought were important problems for students in general (not necessarily for themselves). Thus the phrasing of the question appears to greatly influence the findings in these investigations.

In conclusion our findings support those of others, particularly Carney and Barak (1974), who found vocational concerns to be the issues needing the greatest attention for most students. Further, our data when examined by subgroups, are also similar to the findings of Kramer, Berger and Miller (1974) in that married students reported the most divergent needs. We also found that women reported more psychosocial concerns than did men, as did Weissberg, Berentsen, Cote, Cravey and Heath (1982). However, the most important needs expressed by all women as a group were also career-related.

Apparently, agencies designed to serve the majority of students must be prepared to address vocational and educational concerns as well as psychosocial problems.

APPENDIX I

NEEDS ASSESSMENT

MEAN RATINGS BY ALL RESPONDENTS
(N ¾ 347, MEAN AGE ¾ 21.44)

		Rating
1.	Choosing my major	2.61
2.	Finding written information about careers and educational programs	3.18
3.	Understanding my interests, skills, values and personality	3.49
4.	Planning my career or vocation	3.63
5.	Improving my study skills	2.68
6.	Managing my time effectively	3.07
7.	Making decisions and solving problems	3.14
8.	Assertively standing up for myself	2.97
9.	Communicating more effectively	3.23
10.	Developing my leadership skills	2.91
11.	Overcoming my fears about speaking in public or in groups	2.66

12. Coping with the stresses in my life	3.31
13. Overcoming my fears about taking tests	2.06
14. Controlling my weight	2.15
15. Controlling my smoking	1.36
16. Resolving disagreements with others	2.46
17. Dealing with obstacles to completing a dissertation	2.03
18. Understanding and coping with loneliness	2.40
19. Interacting with people of the opposite sex	2.66
20. Developing my helping skills (listening, communicating, caring, etc.)	2.99
21. Being part of a two career couple	2.82
22. Coping with a handicap	1.68
23. Exploring my marital expectations	2.78
24. Setting reasonable expectations for myself	3.26
25. Improving my relationships with others	3.05
26. Developing self confidence and self-esteem	3.00
27. Getting myself energized to tackle my goals	3.05
28. Dealing with a problem pregnancy	1.75
29. Making choices about my sexual behavior	2.45
30. Clarifying my values	2.73
31. Increasing my control of drug usage	1.40
32. Increasing my control of alcohol usage	1.57
33. Dealing with alcohol or drug users	2.16
34. Coping with sadness or depression	2.76
35. Coping with my separation or divorce	1.48
36. Dealing with a death	2.23
37. Dealing with my parents' divorce or separation	1.62

38. Becoming more independent   2.27
39. Coping with the end of a   2.46
    relationship
40. Enriching a relationship I have   3.11
41. Dealing with male/female stereotypes   2.34
42. Combining family and school/career   2.65
43. Finding and enjoying leisure time   2.84
44. Making friends   2.66
45. Coping with issues of being in a couple   2.62
46. Lessening procrastination   3.04
47. Dealing with homesickness   1.56
48. Learning to live with roommates   1.99
49. Handling competition   2.43
50. Dealing with concerns about homosexual   1.66
    issues
51. Dealing with concerns about heterosexual   2.38
    issues
52. Other   2.44

REFERENCES

1. Carney, C. G., and Barak, A.: A survey of student needs and student personnel services. *Journal of College Student Personnel, 17*(4):280-284, 1976.
2. Flores, T. R.: Student personnel programs for married students: a needs assessment. *Journal of College Student Personnel, 16*(2):154-159, 1978.
3. Henggeler, S. W., Sallis, J. F., and Cooper, P. F.: Comparison of university mental health needs priorities identified by professionals and students. *Journal of Counseling Psychology, 27*(2):217-219, 1980.
4. Indrisano, V. E., and Auerbach, S. M.: Mental health needs assessment of a major urban university. *Journal of the American College Health Association, 27*(4):205-209, 1979.
5. Kramer, H. C., Berger, F., and Miller, G.: Student concerns and sources of assistance. *Journal of College Student Personnel, 15*(5):389-393, 1974.
6. Rue, P., and Lawler, A.: Psychological services needs assessment (Counseling Center Project). University of North Carolina at Chapel Hill, unpublished questionnaire, 1980.
7. Talley, J. E., Barrow, J. C., Fulkerson, K. F., and Moore, C. A.: A compari-

son of telephone *vs.* mail strategies in conducting a university psychological services needs assessment. *Journal of American College Health, 32*(3):101-103, 1983.

8. Weissberg, M., Berentsen, M., Cote, A., Cravey, B., and Heath, K.: An assessment of the personal, career, and academic needs of undergraduate students. *Journal of College Student Personnel, 23*(2):115-122, 1982.

Chapter III.

THE DEVELOPMENT OF AN INTEGRATED MULTIDISCIPLINARY SERVICE AT DUKE UNIVERSITY

JANE CLARK MOORMAN

Introduction

IN 1977 Duke University established a consolidated center to pro-vide its students with a comprehensive range of psychological, psychiatric, and developmental services. The new agency, called Counseling and Psychological Services (CAPS), developed out of an organizational merger of the Student Mental Health Service and the University Counseling Center. From its beginning CAPS has uti-lized an integrated multidisciplinary model of service delivery by clinical and counseling psychologists, clinical social workers, and psychiatrists working closely together as a team. This approach was designed to meet the related needs of individual students for psycho-social counseling and psychotherapy, vocational counseling and ca-reer planning services, and educational programming. In order to explain how our model developed, I will describe the underlying philosophical and theoretical perspective that guided these efforts, the merger process, the resultant pattern of staffing and services, and the vitally important cross-fertilization of disciplines. Finally, the advantages and disadvantages of this model will be addressed.

PHILOSOPHICAL AND THEORETICAL
PERSPECTIVE

Few educators today would challenge the idea that higher education involves more than gaining significant knowledge and intellectual competence. But what else should it involve, and what responsibility does a college or university have to provide its students with broader opportunities? Increasing budgetary constraints, coupled with the anticipated decline in full-time student enrollment that colleges and universities face throughout the next decade, create a critical need for strategies to streamline both services and costs. The duplication resulting from separate units for student mental health and for counseling has already been cause for administrative review on a number of campuses. Such reviews are likely to increase over the next few years. While acknowledging the continuing importance of controlling costs, it is equally important to recognize that bringing together vocational counseling, career planning, psychosocial counseling, and psychiatric services may provide other significant advantages both for the institution and, most importantly, for the student.

Many writers have described the developmental tasks characteristic of late adolescence and early adulthood, the period through which most college students are passing. Despite the variety of perspectives employed, the literature reflects broad agreement that, in addition to building intellectual competence, five other facets of personal development are of primary importance: separating psychologically from one's family, achieving a sexual identity, formulating a personal value system, developing the capacity for intimacy, and establishing a path for career development. While these different facets of an individual's personal development can be treated separately for descriptive purposes, clearly they do not occur one at a time or in any given sequence. Indeed, the student seems to be involved in all of these tasks more or less simultaneously as the many experiences with family, peers, teachers and other significant adults in life are gradually integrated. The degree to which each individual is able to analyze and synthesize these experiences in a self-affirming yet realistic fashion will affect significantly the goals s/he sets and the values governing the individual's efforts to attain them. Indeed, this process largely determines the level of personal maturity one is able to achieve.

Influential writers on the developmental process who are concerned especially with the young adult agree that late adolescence — the college years — is a critical period. For example, in his book *Identity: Youth and Crisis*, Erikson (1968) defines crisis as a necessary turning point. Using "crisis" in the same sense, Coons (1971) observes that ". . . crises are the rule rather than the exception for college students." In his important study, *On Adolescence: A Psychoanalytic Interpretation*, Blos describes late adolescence as "a decisive turning point, and consequently a time of crisis, which so often overtaxes the integrative capacity of the individual and results in adaptive failures, ego deformations, defensive maneuvers, and severe psychopathology" (Coons, 1971).

Experienced college mental health professionals have become increasingly aware that the normal, but often difficult, developmental tasks which challenge the university-age student are indeed inextricably intertwined with one another in the student's personal development. Furthermore, these tasks often significantly affect how students handle the formal education process aimed at intellectual development. A typical example will illustrate the complexity of college students' developmental concerns.

A familiar phenomenon on today's campus is a young man in conflict due to pressure from his father who wants the son to follow him in the practice of medicine even though that young man's interest in and fitness for medical school are in doubt. Such a student must first achieve a sense of psychological separation from his father before he will be able to resist this subtle yet steady pressure appropriately and without guilt or anxiety. Depending upon the severity of the young man's conflict, his efforts to resolve these concerns may be enhanced by one or more of the following services:

1. Brief counseling or psychotherapy to assist conflict resolution.
2. Vocational interest testing and interpretation that is designed to open up other vocational options for consideration.
3. If the level of anxiety is high, evaluation by a psychiatrist to determine whether medication and/or hospitalization is appropriate.

The more quickly the student is able to resolve his concerns, the earlier his psychic energies will be free to be channeled once again into the pursuit of academic achievement and personal happiness.

The logic of the situation calls for grouping together naturally related services that students, like this young man, may need from time to time in working toward the accomplishment of their developmental tasks. Why should they have to go to two or more offices in various parts of the campus for multiple evaluations in order to seek psychotherapy, vocational counseling, career planning services, and a medication evaluation? The relevant professionals joined together in an integrated multidisciplinary team can provide rapid and effective services focusing on the student as a whole, unique person, rather than on just one facet of the student's concern. Our experience at Duke has convinced me that such a team serves students more effectively than separate staffs that are unable to collaborate in developing a comprehensive plan designed to address the several facets of a given student's concern.

The comprehensive student service at Duke University called Counseling and Psychological Services, or CAPS, came into being in part as an expression of the University's philosophy of education, a philosophy based on its commitment to the holistic development of the individual student. No one has expressed this commitment more eloquently than Duke's first president, Dr. William Preston Few. Speaking to an early graduating class, he said:

> Everywhere in the University, but especially in the undergraduate college, we are trying to break down departmentalizing walls and make the subjects exist for the student and not the student for the subjects; that is, make the student the unit . . . .
> Duke University must [provide] . . . an education that seeks to liberate all the powers and develop all the capacity of our human nature. We are aware that we have set a high and difficult goal to attain; but it is a goal worth all our striving (Few, 1931, p. 196).

Devising effective ways to work toward this goal is far more difficult than simply espousing it. Many institutions — Duke among them — have proclaimed this commitment only to fall far short of the objective in actual practice. From our experience at CAPS we have discovered that it is possible to implement a program of comprehensive psychological services consistent with the University's objective of the holistic development of students.

BACKGROUND OF THE MERGER

In their creation of CAPS during the mid-seventies, Duke administrators renewed the University's commitment to the whole student expressed by Dr. Few nearly fifty years earlier. Cognizant of the close relationship between the developmental tasks students face, they sought to provide them with effective support services. The University administrators became convinced that the optimal way to meet students' needs would be through close collaboration among professionals of different disciplines seeking to help students achieve the highest level of maturity and personal satisfaction possible.

Impetus for further planning was provided by the Southern Association of Colleges and Schools Review Committee which visited the University during the fall of 1976 for its decennial accreditation review. This Committee recommended that the University "study professional counseling services . . . to increase their effectiveness" (The Committee on Counseling Services, 1977, p. 1). The University responded to this recommendation by establishing a study committee which worked through the spring of 1977 exploring ways to strengthen counseling services at Duke. In its report this committee proposed merging the University Counseling Center and the Student Mental Health Service to form the core of a new service. The committee sketched out a plan for the new organization and as the central thrust of its recommendation reaffirmed the University's commitment to a philosophy of individual student development:

> As an educational facility the University is obligated to provide the services necessary to maximize the potential of its student body. From this perspective, Duke University is dedicated to furnishing a full scope of counseling services with the realization that these services should share an extremely close tie with all the other educational aspects of the University. The common goal of the educational and counseling activities should be to contribute to the development and personality growth of all students at Duke, not just those representing an extreme of maladaptive behavior. . . . The proposed reorganization . . . would provide a high quality, centrally located facility [staffed by] . . . a group of professionals whose training and expertise vary widely and who . . . would have the collective capacity to assist students in dealing with a wide range of vocational, educational, and social-psychological problems (The Committee on Counseling Services, 1977, p.5-6).

The distinctive character of CAPS at Duke lies, therefore, in the combination of principle and practice. Its philosophy holds that not only are developmental tasks of students closely intertwined, but services provided to help them accomplish these tasks should likewise be closely integrated if the goal of their holistic development is to be realized. To my knowledge, CAPS' closely integrated multidisciplinary team approach to the delivery of student services, including psychosocial counseling, psychiatric care, vocational counseling, career planning, and educational programming is a configuration of staff and services unique among university programs.

Although there are several articles describing the merger of a college or university counseling program with its student health service, a review of the literature reveals no publications about the formation of a service as comprehensive as CAPS. Schwartz (1973) describes the integration of a psychologist providing counseling services with the medical staff of the campus health service at a small Oregon instutition, Willamette University. In an article on student participation in the development of health service programming, Klotz and Siegman (1975) focus briefly on the administrative (though not collocational) merger of the Counseling Center and the Student Health Center at the University of Southern California. By far the most comprehensive description of such a merger is given in an article by Foster (1982) describing the organizational merger of a "traditional counseling center with a traditional comprehensive student health center's mental health unit" at Indiana University, Bloomington. Otherwise, studies specifically on the consolidation of university counseling centers and student mental health services appear to be absent from the literature.

While it is clear that mergers of various types have taken place at several other institutions such as the University of California at Berkeley and Stanford University, none of them have a consolidated service carrying *primary* responsibility for all four of the major service areas of psychosocial counseling, psychiatric care, vocational counseling and career planning, and educational programming. As we look with foreboding toward declines in student enrollment and increasing budgetary limitations in the 1980's and 1990's, it would not be surprising if such consolidations become more commonplace primarily for practical reasons even if only peripheral attention were given to philosophical considerations.

THE MERGER PROCESS

Prior to the merger, both the University Counseling Center and the Student Mental Health Service at Duke had functioned in fairly traditional ways, with the former handling mainly vocational-educational counseling and testing, and the latter providing largely psychotherapy and medication evaluations. Since the merger of these two offices, CAPS has been the only campus service having the specific purpose of providing counseling for the 9,500 Duke students enrolled in undergraduate, graduate, professional, and allied health programs.

The fact that CAPS is administratively and locationally separate from the Student Health Service may appear contradictory to the University's stated philosophy and CAPS' commitment to providing integrated services. Why are they not consolidated? It was the strong conviction of University administrators that counseling/mental health services for students should include services ranging broadly from psychiatric care of clear psychopathology to educational programming intended to enhance the normal development of all students and prevent serious psychological problems where possible. They wanted CAPS to be recognized by students primarily as a *developmental resource* for *all students*, not just those having "serious problems." They wanted utilization of mental health services to be viewed as a *normative* part of student life. The Student Health Service had been clearly established as a division of Duke Unversity Medical Center's Department of Community and Family Medicine and was viewed by students as operating in a "medical model" to "treat the sick." For these reasons, it was decided that the director of CAPS should report to Central Administration directly and that CAPS would be centrally but discreetly located on the University campus where it would be easily accessible to all students. During the first two years of operation, CAPS' director reported to the Provost who was closely involved in the initial phase of development; however, in 1979 a reorganization of the University's administrative structure led to the appointment of a Vice-President for Student Affairs to whom the director of CAPS has reported since.

The directors of the Student Health Service and CAPS have continued both formal and informal liaisons and in serving students the two staffs continually collaborate consultatively and through referrals. In addition, CAPS staff members have admitting privileges at the University Infirmary and work closely with its staff in treating students admitted for psychological reasons.

PATTERN OF STAFFING AND SERVICES

The configuration of CAPS' staffing and services is one that evolved gradually during the early years of operation. The principal mandate given CAPS from its beginning was one of providing a range of integrated services to students. A standard of excellence has functioned as the guiding principle both in the evolution of the staffing pattern and program development. Thus, a highly qualified professional staff was employed initially to develop the services.

It was clear from the beginning that the Unviersity's optimal benefit from such a program could be achieved only through close collaborative planning by the University administration and CAPS' director during the initial phase of its development. With this in mind, they very early evolved together a plan for anticipated staffing needs over the first five years based on their determination of general program priorities and a mutual understanding of the fiscal commitment necessary each year.

The initial staff consisted of five and one-half full-time equivalent psychologists, psychiatrists, and clinical social workers. Currently, the staffing pattern includes two full-time clinical social workers (who serve as director and assistant director), two full-time counseling psychologists, one full-time clinical psychologist, two half-time psychiatrists, and one half-time clinical social worker. Each has a faculty appointment in the Department of Psychiatry of Duke University Medical Center or in the University's Department of Psychology.

Criteria for selection of the multidisciplinary staff included not only clinical expertise but interest and skills in consultation and educational programming within the University community as well as in training and research related to the development of university students. In addition, enthusiasm for building a comprehensive service through interdisciplinary collaboration and a desire to broaden one's own skills by understanding other perspectives on student development were considered essential. It has been the rule, rather than the exception, among the staff to accord equal respect to varying kinds of expertise; respect for other professional disciplines has become a valued and important principle of professional practice in the eyes of both staff and those in training at CAPS.

The senior staff is complemented by advanced students in three mental health disciplines who participate in CAPS' Training Program. During the first year of operation, there were only three part-time professionals in training, one in clinical social work and two in psychiatry totaling one full-time equivalent position. Since the fifth year of operation there have been seven trainee positions including three fourth-year psychiatric residents (one-quarter time each), one second-year master's level clinical social work trainee (three-fifths time), and three full-time predoctoral interns in clinical and counseling psychology. Thus the presence of professionals-in-training on the staff total four and one-third full-time equivalents, bringing the overall professional staff configuration to nearly eleven full-time equivalents. Not only has the Training Program fulfilled a major initial goal of CAPS, to provide advanced multidisciplinary training in the mental health professions with an indepth exposure to college mental health services; those in training have also provided the staff capability to broaden services, given the limited size of CAPS' senior staff. Clearly, excellence in service and in advanced training should go hand-in-hand, and the senior staff's involvement in both has provided them a stimulating and rewarding balance of professional activities.

Services offered by CAPS include evaluation, crisis intervention, and brief individual counseling/psychotherapy regarding psychosocial, vocational and educational concerns; other vocational planning services; couples and group counseling; psychiatric evaluations for medication and hospitalization; referral services; seminars on academic, personal, and social skills development; and a broad range of testing services. In addition to these direct services for students, the staff is actively involved in campus life through consultation and outreach educational programming. All senior staff participate actively in CAPS' Training Program through both supervision and didactic presentations and are involved in research activities as well.

THE ORGANIZATIONAL MATRIX

The administrative organization of CAPS is a simple one consisting of the Director, Assistant Director, and Coordinating Committee. The Committee is composed of the five full-time staff members who carry responsibility for coordinating activities in the following areas: clinical services; vocational planning, educational programming, and testing services; consultation; training; research and program evaluation.

Given the wide variety of functions carried out within the CAPS framework, naturally all disciplines do not participate in every activity. The specific training and skills unique to each discipline represented on the staff are fully utilized, but beyond these considerable flexibility is accorded each staff member to learn about and help provide other types of services offered by the agency. The staff's efforts to move beyond the stereotypic role often assigned the various mental health professions by society is demonstrated by the activities of one psychiatrist who, over the past few years, has not only provided a full range of clinical services, supervision, and teaching but has also led a structured group on stress management, served as co-facilitator for staff planning retreats, and assumed the roles of instructor and comic entertainer in resident advisor training. While some of these activities require no psychiatric training *per se*, they have served to reduce the stigma so often attached to psychological services by allowing professionals to be perceived as less threatening human beings who are concerned about and interested in all aspects of student life. Such involvement in University life through these kinds of consultation and educational activities has been important in significantly integrating CAPS into the thinking of members of the University community as a resource for all students and those who work with them. The strict policy of confidentiality to which CAPS adheres has in no way been compromised by this. Rather, it has seemingly become a cornerstone of the students' confidence in the services offered by CAPS which has been reflected in their increasing utilization of the services during the first five years of operation.

As discussed earlier, the distinctive character of CAPS stems both from the unusually broad range of its functions (psychosocial, vocational and educational counseling as well as career planning and psychiatric services) and from the markedly different professional backgrounds of the staff working together as a team.

While all professional staff participate in most of the traditional clinical and consultation services, the vocational counseling and testing services are provided principally by counseling psychologists and psychology interns. Though many of the developmentally oriented structured group seminars and workshops are led by the psychology staff and interns, clinical social work and psychiatry staff are also involved in educational programming. All medication and hospitalization evaluations are provided by psychiatrists and psychiatric residents. All staff, however, are involved in teaching and supervising professionals in training in their own as well as other disciplines.

While it is clear that no psychological services program functions well without a well-trained support staff, I must underscore the key role of all our support staff in CAPS' development. Our clinic service coordinator, staff assistant/office manager and secretary have not only performed their regular duties with marked sensitivity and dedication; they have also contributed creative ideas for improving services and routine office operations that are indicative of their strong commitment to excellence. Their contributions from the beginning of CAPS have been indeed central to the progressive development of the program.

CROSS-FERTILIZATION

The process of cross-fertilization among the various disciplines in university mental health services and counseling centers is not one routinely addressed. In a review of the literature no discussions were found suggesting the means by which this often delicate but immensely enriching process can be accomplished. Naturally, the following question arises: In the unique service configuration of CAPS, has cross-fertilization occurred, and if so, how?

During the first year of merged operation, professional staff providing vocational counseling and those providing clinical services, while under "one roof," functioned rather separately. It was not until the second year that the staff, and therefore the services, was truly merged. As professionals of different backgrounds worked together, they began to understand each other better as well as the unique approach each brought to serving students. The diversity of disciplines has not brought about rivalry as a major issue; to the contrary, it has generally served to generate stimulating staff discussion and creative problem-solving. The process of cross-fertilization among disciplines has not been automatic. Rather, it has been a definite, but very gradual, process of molding together an increasingly broad corporate expertise through both formal and informal opportunities for staff interaction.

Formal opportunities for staff to share their various approaches with one another are of several kinds. They include the following: Administrative Staff Meeting, Staff Colloquium, Team Case Conference, Coordinators' Conference, Training Seminar, Conference on Structured Groups and Outreach Education, Consultation Conference, and Staff Retreats. The most important of these opportunities for cross-fertilization is the Team Case Conference. Each of the two teams is composed of seven or eight senior staff members and those in training in all three disciplines who meet one and one-half hours per week to discuss intake evaluations, ongoing cases, and special therapeutic problems. The format is one of rotating the presentation among members and providing mutual consultation and supervision as well as the challenge of sharing and defending theoretical perspectives and interventions utilized. The Administrative Staff Meeting is a biweekly one-hour conference of the full staff that provides a forum for discussion of organizational and campus issues and administrative problem-solving. On alternate weeks the Staff Colloquium is held at this time and provides an ongoing in-service education program for all staff. Presentations on a wide variety of topics relating to the psychological issues of students and their development are given by invited speakers as well as staff members. The Coordinators' Conference is a forum in which the Director and the Program Area Coordinators meet to carry out inter-area collaboration, decision-making, and planning. Ongoing conferences focusing on the development and implementation of structured groups, outreach education, and consultation services meet regularly throughout the academic year for all involved staff.

The Training Seminar is a didactic conferece for professionals in training of all disciplines and interested staff that meets two hours daily during the first month of the academic year and weekly for two hours thereafter. A wide range of topics related to student development and services is taught by the entire senior staff. Though less structured than formal meetings, semi-annual Staff Retreats have become valued occasions for professional staff, those in training, and support staff alike. They are planned by members of the staff for the purposes of promoting staff cohesion, participating in corporate organizational problem-solving and planning, evaluating present policies, programs, and procedures, and assisting staff members in setting and achieving their individual professional goals. While informal opportunities for spontaneous staff interaction such as coffee breaks, staff parties, and *ad hoc* brief consultations need no elaboration, they may well be more important to the development of mutual understanding and *esprit de corps* than any scheduled meetings. Through all these activities staff members of each discipline learn much from each other that helps them understand the often multifaceted concerns of students. While in-depth expertise in disciplines other than one's own is neither claimed nor sought by staff, some overlapping of roles is a natural and beneficial result of cross-fertilization in such a multidisciplinary setting. All staff continually develop a broader as well as a more refined understanding not only of the various facets of students' developmental concerns but also of what kinds of services would be most useful. Therefore, more rapid and effective referrals can be made to colleagues with different expertise in the same office, frequently precluding the multiple evaluations and delay of appropriate services usually involved in external referral of students.

Since the consolidation of programs, our data have shown that an average of 35 percent of the students requesting initial appointments for counseling stated they wanted help with "a vocational concern" while staff members report that 80 percent of counseling hours are focused on "personal" (psychosocial) concerns. The availability of both types of services in the same office appears to have significantly increased the frequency with which this largely pre-professional student body is utilizing campus mental health services.

UTILIZATION OF SERVICES

Comparison of 1976-77 pre-merger combined utilization statistics for the University Counseling Center and the Student Mental Health Service with 1981-82 post-merger data for CAPS strongly substantiates this. The pre-merger data showed that 812 students were seen in 1976-77 in 2,900 service hours in the two offices. In 1981-82, 1,039 students received services at CAPS totalling, 5,746 service hours. These figures represent an approximate 30 percent increase in the number of students seeking services and a 98 percent increase in the number of student service hours over a five-year span following consolidation. This expansion in service-hours reflects a significant increase in both the number of counseling sessions *per se* as well as an increase in career planning and other structured groups offered. The latter types of service have been developed gradually.

With regard to student satisfaction with services, a spring 1982 Client Satisfaction Questionnarie administered to a sample of students using CAPS for psychotherapy/psychosocial counseling gave some indication of this. A scale from one (not at all true) to ten (extremely true) was given for rating items. Item fifteen, "The counselor impressed me as a skilled counselor" had a mean rating of 7.7 while Item sixteen, "In summary I am quite satisfied with the services I received at CAPS" had amean rating of 7.5.

SEQUENCE OF PROGRAMMATIC OBJECTIVES

During the early stages of CAPS' development the staff entered into a strong collaborative effort with the director to clarify the intended parameters of the program, establish clear objectives, set priorities, and implement the program. Given the variety of professional backgrounds represented, such decision-making required not only strong commitment to the multifunctional purpose of the agency, but mutual respect among the staff and a sense of corporate pride in and responsibility for the quality of all services rendered.

The sequence of major program objectives accomplished during the first five years include the following:

Year I:

1. Merging administratively and collocationally the already established services for students provided by the former University Counseling Center and Student Mental Health Service (i.e., psychosocial counseling and psychiatric services, vocational-educational counseling and testing, the national testing program, consultation and training for members of the University community, and training of advanced students in mental health disciplines).

2. Facilitating *esprit de corps* and a high level of moral among the merged staffs.
3. Coordinating the diverse counseling and psychiatric services being merged.
4. Establishing policies and procedures that would accommodate the broad variety of programmatic needs and personnel.
5. Informing the University community of services available through active liaison efforts and publicity as well as seeking its advice through the establishment of three advisory committees: the Committee on Professional Standards, the Student Advisory Committee, and the General Advisory Committee.
6. Setting long-range program goals and priorities for the merged service.
7. Planning annual and long-range budgets based on program goals and priorities.

Year II:

1. Employment of a third staff psychologist with the primary responsibility of establishing and directing a predoctoral psychology internship program.
2. Delegation of administrative responsibility to five coordinators for the following program areas: clinical services; consultation; vocational counseling, educational programming, and testing; training; research and program evaluation.
3. Improvement of career planning services.
   a. Development of vocational planning structured groups/seminars.
   b. Reorganization and expansion of the career planning library resources.

Year III:

1. Appointment of the Assistant Director.
2. Implementation of the Psychology Internship Program with the selection and training of the first two interns.
3. Development of a strong outreach education component.
4. Development of ongoing in-service education through staff colloquia.

Year IV:

1. Significant increase in research development, writing, and presentations by staff members at professional meetings.
2. Preparation for and initiation of accreditation review process by American Psychological Association of CAPS' Internship Training Program in Clinical and Counseling Psychology.

Year V:

1. Full accreditation of Internship Program in Clinical Psychology and Counseling Psychology by the American Psychological Association.
2. Expansion of the Internship Program with the addition of a third full-time intern position and a part-time supervising senior psychologist.

The establishment of a comprehensive service such as CAPS is a complex process whether accomplished through merger or not. It cannot happen quickly. It is, and must be, a gradual process if it is to have lasting effectiveness because the planning, negotiating, coordinating, and dovetailing of various programs and kinds of expertise take considerable time. All these processes require adjustment to a myriad of operational changes by staff and university alike.

ADVANTAGES AND DISADVANTAGES OF A CONSOLIDATED SERVICE

A review of our consolidated service after five years of operation reveals a number of advantages and potential disadvantages that merit discussion. The inclusion of developmental services traditionally more acceptable to use, such as vocational counseling and skills development seminars, with psychosocial counseling and psychiatric services, to which our society clearly attaches a significant stigma, has raised the comfort level of many students in seeking the latter kinds of services. As stated earlier, far more students request an initial appointment for "vocational counseling" than actually deal with these issues as central concerns in the counseling process. This is viewed as a major advantage of the consolidation of services because it makes it easier for students who find it difficult to seek psychotherapy directly, for whatever reason, to establish contact with a professional counselor for an "acceptable" reason; the counselor can then, if indicated, refer them for services within CAPS such as a medication evaluation, a bulimia group, or psychiatric treatment for the management of psychiatric illness.

Having comprehensive services located together underscores the normalcy of the closely related developmental tasks students face and precludes their having to make an arbitrary decision as to where to seek help. Similarly, confusion among faculty, staff, and resident advisors as to where to refer a student needing psychological assistance has been virtually eliminated.

Another advantage is the improved staff effectiveness gained through close collaboration, fostering in each staff member a better understanding of the expertise of colleagues and their approach to serving students. This mutual respect and understanding greatly facilitate and expedite helpful referrals among colleagues who work closely together daily. As a result, students tend not to "slip between the cracks" as often.

Reducing duplication in services and at the same time broadening and improving the quality and range of services represents a major asset. While such a model is clearly not appropriate for every campus, in middle-sized universities such as Duke where we serve approximately 10,000 students, the staff needed in psychological services is likely to be large enough to incorporate enough diversity of background to be stimulating for senior staff and professionals in training while at the same time small enough to allow close collaboration and cross-fertilization among disciplines. Both of these aspects of our staffing pattern have proven most effective and satisfying.

Potential disadvantages also need to be considered. First, friction and competition which often exist in multidisciplinary staffs are potentially a major risk of this model. It has not been a significant problem in our experience probably due in part to very careful staff recruitment in which a high premium was placed on commitment to interdisciplinary delivery of comprehensive services. Second, with any organizational merger there is always the danger of unrealistic expectations for either achieving significantly increased service with the same staff or for maintaining adequate service with a reduced staff. Such expectations can be avoided or diminished to an acceptable level by close collaboration between university administrators and mental health professionals throughout the planning process. Third, on campuses located in areas where mental health resources are quite limited, merger of the counseling center and the mental health service could be perceived by students to further limit their choices; however, that is not the case at Duke with its medical center adjoining the campus and a wide variety of mental health professionals in private practice.

A fourth disadvantage is that reorganization always exacts a temporary toll in the form of reduced staff effectiveness growing out of resentment and insecurity due to the changes in operating routines, in personal expectations, indeed in organizational goals. These changes also add up to a very demanding and complex administrative load thrust upon the chief administrator during the early years of consolidation. Duke did not avoid this pitfall but its impact was rendered tolerable by the goodwill that was widely shared and the promise of improved service. Patience, sometimes defined as an awareness that "things take time," came very slowly; but it did come in the form of recognition that accomplishing program goals must be an *evolving* process.

The integrated multidisciplinary model utilized in CAPS' development has worked well at Duke University. Staff members have cultivated a richer holistic perspective on student needs and more clearly embraced a developmental model of prevention and treatment. All have experienced some blending of roles as they have gradually broadened their own professional skills and functions. A high level of stability in personnel has greatly facilitated mutual trust and cohesion among the staff. We have found one result of this to be that momentum continues to build as energy is freed for learning and creativity in providing services and developing programs. Fragmentation and duplication have been largely overcome; separate services are no longer competing for funds. Staff of all disciplines are united in their efforts to meet the various facets of students' needs; and most important, students' increased utilization of and satisfaction with consolidated services have been marks of the effectiveness of the CAPS' model. I believe the result of consolidation of services on our campus has been what all helping professionals in higher education seek, i.e., improved services for our students.

REFERENCES

1. *Ad Hoc* Committee on Counseling Services: *Final Report and Recommendations April, 1977*. The Committee, Durham, Duke University [Mimeographed], p. 1, 5-6, 1977.
2. Coons, F. W.: The developmental tasks of the college student. In Feinstein, S. C., Giovacchini, P., and Miller, A. A. (Eds.): *Adolescent Psychiatry*. New York, Basic Books, 1971, vol. I, pp. 257, 258.
3. Erikson, E. H.: *Identity: Youth and Crisis*. New York, Norton, 1968.
4. Few, W. P.: Address to the graduating class of 1931. In *Alumni Register of Duke University*, Durham, Department of Alumni Affairs, Duke University, June, 1931, p. 196.
5. Foster, T. V.: Merger 1980: the organizational integration of college mental health services. *Journal of American College Health*, 30(4):171-174, 1982.
6. Klotz, A. L., and Siegman, A.: Strategies for delivering human services to college students in a student-participant program. *Journal of the American College Health Association*, 23(3):233-237, 1975.
7. Schwartz, R. K.: Integration of medical and counseling services. *Personnel and Guidance Journal*, 51(5):347-349, 1973.

Chapter IV.

THE ZUNG SELF-RATING DEPRESSION SCALE AS AN INTAKE SCREENING INSTRUMENT

JOHN C. BARROW, JOSEPH E. TALLEY,
KAREN H. MILLER AND WILLIAM W. K. ZUNG

THE era of accountability has arrived for university student mental health and counseling centers. Most centers are experiencing heavy demands from students undergoing psychosocial and academic-vocational difficulties. In fact, lengthy waiting lists are the rule rather than the exception. In addition, student mental health and counseling centers are increasingly being expected to provide multiple services to their campus communities. As well as being asked to provide remedial counseling and therapy services they are being expected to assume greater roles in consultative and educative activities designed to prevent the formation of serious psychological problems and to aid students in progressing in normal developmental tasks. Unfortunately, it appears unlikely that very many student mental health or counseling services can realistically hope to meet these increased demands through the acquisition of new staff resources. The use of procedures that contribute to the efficiency with which students receive services is therefore desirable.

One area in which mental health and counseling centers can

work to improve efficiency is the intake and screening process. In view of the heavy case loads characteristic of the services, it is important that the professional proceed quickly with conceptualizing students' problems, identifying the degree and kind of psychopathology respresented, clarifying students' needs, and formulating plans for disposition and intervention. One important area to assess is the degree of depression shown by a student and the nature of the depressive symptoms, including the physiological concommitants. The consequences of failure to identify the presence of depression are potentially quite serious. Yet the signs can easily be overlooked, particularly in relatively intelligent and verbal university students who may appear more in command of emotional processes than they actually are. In light of these reasons, we have experimented with including the Zung Self-Rating Depression Scale (See Table I) in our standard intake procedures.

The purpose of this chapter is to discuss our intake approach. First, we will provide more information on the importance of accurately assessing depression at intake. Second, the screening procedures and the Zung instrument will be described. Third, a study examining this instrument's ability to discriminate a clinical from a non-clinical group of students will be presented. Fourth, further discussion and final recommendations will be offered to other professionals interested in using similar approaches.

THE NEED FOR SCREENING PROCEDURES FOR DEPRESSION

Depression is a frequently occurring problem among university students. The rate of depression in this group has been found to be as much as 50 percent higher than the rate in other Americans between the ages of eleven and seventy-four (Bumberry, McClure, and Oliver, 1978). In another study a random sample of sophomores was asked to complete a retrospective version of the Beck Depression Inventory for the preceding college year, their first at college. Seventy-five percent of those who responded had experienced depression in a mild, if not more severe form (Bosse, Croghan, and Greenstein, 1975).

A large number of students reporting to mental health and counseling centers experience depression. Of those evaluated at one student mental health center, approximately 25 percent were found to have significant depressive symptoms (Brown, 1978). A review of records of 578 students seen at another student mental health center found a 43.6 percent prevalence of clinical depression. Almost half of these depressed students seemed to experience a depression associated with difficulty with late adolescent and early adult development issues (O'Neil, and Marziali, 1978). When therapists at our Service were asked to identify the primary affective problem for students treated, depression was selected for 24 percent (Talley, 1983). Thus, the accumulated evidence suggests that mild depression may occur in up to 75 percent of students and that more problematic, clinical depression occurs in approximately 25 percent of students using mental health services.

When students do experience depression, it can have several adverse effects. Academic functioning can be hampered by depression. Whitney, Cadoret, and McClure (1971) used standardized test scores to control for innate academic ability in examining the relationship of depression with academic performance. Students who were depressed at the beginning of a semester obtained lower grade point averages and had a greater incidence of withdrawal from courses than students who were not depressed.

As well as acting as a negative influence in students' academic lives, depression can interfere with social development. Social withdrawal, irritability, and a devaluing of self and others are known to accompany depressed feelings (Beck, Rush, Shaw, and Emery, 1979). Depressed studens may be less able to adapt to changing circumstances and to cope with threatening or unexpected situations than undepressed students. Hammen and Cochran (1981) commented on the relationship of depression with increased emotional upset and sense of insecurity in college students' responses to stressful situations. In light of the negative impact of depression on the academic, social and emotional well-being of university students, Whitney, Cadoret, and McClure (1971) suggested that early detection and treatment of depression can help prevent the waste of college resources.

An additional reason for the development of procedures for early identification of depression is its association with suicide. While recent studies have suggested the incidence of college student suicide to be less dramatic than once believed (Heinrichs, 1980; Kraft, 1980; Schwartz, and Reifler, 1980), the assessment of suicidal potential remains a crucial and necessary skill for student mental health and counseling professionals. Students committing suicide during a twenty year period were studied at the University of Massachusetts (Kraft, 1980). Some rather striking findings were that 58 percent had previously sought mental health treatment and that 37 percent had seen a mental health professional less than one week prior to death. Although simply obtaining service at a mental health agency does not necessarily prevent attempts at suicide, it stands to reason that an accurate assessment of the degree and nature of depression during the intake process may increase the probability of suicide prevention.

THE ZUNG SELF-RATING DEPRESSION SCALE (SDS) AS AN INTAKE INSTRUMENT

In view of the importance of accurate and efficient assessment of depression in students seeking counseling and mental health services, use of the Zung Self-Rating Depression Scale (Zung, 1965) was incorporated into our intake procedures. Prior to their first visit with a member of our staff, students are asked to complete the Zung instrument, along with an intake form consisting of demographic information.

The Zung instrument was selected for several reasons. First, its psychometric properties have been well studied (Zung, 1965; Zung, Richards, and Short, 1965). Second, it is relatively brief, consisting of twenty items, and is therefore less disconcerting to students than a lengthier instruments might be. Third, its format is simple and clearly designed, making it relatively easy to answer even by students preoccupied with problems. Fourth, it is quickly and reliably scored, a factor that is important for a busy counseling or student mental health center, in that time pressures are as heavily experienced by support staff members as by the mental health practitioners.

Each of the twenty items in the Zung Self-Rating Depression Scale describes a symptom or correlate of depression. Students are asked to respond to each item on a scale of one to four, with one indicating that the symptom is experienced "none or a little of the time" and four indicating it is experienced "most or all of the time." The individual item scores are summated to a single score (range twenty to eighty) that may then be "converted" to the SDS Index ranging from twenty-five to one hundred.

Prior to the first intake session, our therapists review a student's Zung along with the intake form containing demographic information. Attention is paid to the SDS Index, in that scores greater than or equal to fifty have been found suggestive of the clinical diagnosis of depression (Zung, 1965). As well as using the overall score our staff members may attend to responses on individual items and/or clusters of items. The symptoms described on the Zung Depression Scale were drawn from three categories: "pervasive affect," "psysiological equivalents," or "psychological equivalents." The rated frequency of the "physiological" items as compared with the "psychological" items can help in assessment of the degree to which the depression may be biologically based. Depending upon the student, therapists may use the Zung information solely for their own conceptualizing or use the instrument as a vehicle for discussion of the student's feelings and difficulties. Administering the Zung prior to the session can reduce the amount of interview time required in making an accurate assessment and can allow the therapist to select important themes or items from the instrument for more thorough review. Students who are reticent or are not particularly introspective or psychologically minded can often discuss their feelings more freely and productively after completing the Zung scale.

THE ZUNG'S CAPACITY TO DISCRIMINATE BETWEEN CLINICAL AND NON-CLINICAL SAMPLES

Our staff members have subjectively reported use of the Zung Self-Rating Depression Scale as an intake instrument to be helpful in assessment of students. However, we thought it important to carry out an objective examination of certain questions regarding the Zung scale, in order to more completely evaluate its value to us. One important issue is whether such an instrument helps differenti-

Table I

ZUNG SELF-RATING DEPRESSION SCALE

	None or a little of the time	Some of the time	Good part of the time	Most or all of the time
1. I feel down-hearted and blue				
2. Morning is when I feel the best				
3. I have crying spells or feel like it				
4. I have trouble sleeping at night				
5. I eat as much as I used to				
6. I still enjoy sex				
7. I notice that I am losing weight				
8. I have trouble with constipation				
9. My heart beats faster than usual				
10. I get tired for no reason				
11. My mind is as clear as it used to be				
12. I find it easy to do the things I used to				
13. I am restless and can't keep still				
14. I feel hopeful about the future				
15. I am more irritable than usual				
16. I find it easy to make decisions				
17. I feel that I am useful and needed				
18. My life is pretty full				
19. I feel that others would be better off if I were dead				
20. I still enjoy the things I used to do				

ate those with "clinically significant" problems from those with problems of a lesser degree. Dr. Zung has provided some evidence regarding the discriminate validity of this instrument. The mean SDS Index of normal controls has been found to be thirty-three, in comparison with means of seventy-four for depressed hospitalized patients and sixty-four for depressed outpatients. The mean scores for patients with clinical disorders other than depression, including anxiety reactions and personality disorders, have also been higher than the mean for normal controls (Zung, 1965; Zung, Richards, and Short, 1965). However, whether the Zung instrument could discriminate between university students who seek service at student mental health and counseling centers from a non-presenting control sample of students had not been investigated. We therefore undertook to compare Zung scores of students using our Service with those obtained from a control sample of students at our university who had not sought help.

The clinical sample consisted of a self-referred group of 431 undergraduate students presenting to our Counseling and Psychological Services Center. These data were obtained in the last half of the 1979-80 academic year and the entire 1980-81 school year. As is our procedure, these students took the Zung along with our demographic intake form prior to meeting with a professional for the first time. The non-clinical control sample consisted of 388 students enrolled in an introductory psychology course. These students completed the Zung instrument along with a brief demographic questionnarie.

The characteristics of subjects in the control sample were found to parallel those of the clinical subjects with one major exception. The control sample was comprised of 59 percent males and 41 percent females. Like most student mental health and counseling centers, our Service is frequented by a higher percentage of females than males. Therefore, our clinical sample contained 37 percent males and 63 percent females. The control sample also appeared to contain a higher percentage of sophomores and a lower percentage of freshman than our clinical sample; however, this difference did not reach statistical significance.

The results are presented in Table II. Differences between groups on the SDS Index and individual items were examined by t-tests. The mean Index score for the clinical sample is clearly higher than the mean for the control sample. The mean Index of 52.2 for the clinical sample is within the range suggested by Zung to be potentially indicative of the presence of depression. A statistically significant difference between the clinical and control samples was also found with eighteen of the twenty individual items. It is interesting that the two items for which differences were *not* found concerned appetite ("I eat as much as I used to") and weight loss ("I notice that I am losing weight").

Table II

COMPARISON OF SELF-RATING DEPRESSION SCALE (SDS)
ITEMS AND INDICES BETWEEN CONTROL
AND CLINICAL POPULATIONS

SDS Item	Control Population Mean (SD)	Clinical Population Mean (SD)	P
Depressed mood	1.7 ± 0.7	2.3 ± 0.8	.001
Diurnal variation	2.4 ± 0.9	2.9 ± 0.9	.001
Crying spells	1.2 ± 0.5	1.9 ± 0.8	.001
Sleep disturbance	1.4 ± 0.7	1.9 ± 1.0	.001
Decreased appetite	1.9 ± 1.1	2.1 ± 1.1	NS
Decreased libido	1.3 ± 0.5	2.1 ± 1.0	.001
Decreased weight	1.5 ± 0.8	1.5 ± 0.8	NS
Constipation	1.1 ± 0.4	1.3 ± 0.6	.001
Tachycardia	1.3 ± 0.5	1.6 ± 0.8	.001
Increased fatigue	1.3 ± 0.6	2.0 ± 0.9	.001
Confusion	1.4 ± 0.8	2.4 ± 1.1	.001
Psychomotor retardation	1.3 ± 0.7	2.4 ± 1.1	.001
Psychomotor agitation	1.9 ± 0.9	2.1 ± 0.9	.001
Hopelessness	1.4 ± 0.7	2.5 ± 1.0	.001
Irritability	1.3 ± 0.6	2.1 ± 0.9	.001
Indecisiveness	1.8 ± 0.9	2.8 ± 0.9	.001
Personal devaluation	1.6 ± 0.8	2.6 ± 1.0	.001
Emptiness	1.4 ± 0.6	2.2 ± 0.9	.001
Suicidal ruminations	1.1 ± 0.4	2.2 ± 0.9	.001
Dissatisfaction	1.4 ± 0.7	2.2 ± 1.0	.001
Index	37.1 ± 7.2	52.2 ± 11.6	.001

The fact that our clinical and control samples had differed in the proportion of males and females makes important the examination of sex differences in the data. Using t-tests, no statistical differences in the SDS Index for male versus females were found in either the control or clinical samples. In the control sample, the mean SDS Index was 36.5 (S.D. = 7.4) for males and 37.8 (S.D. = 6.9) for females. In the clinical sample, the SDS Index was 53.2 (S.D. = 11.6) for males and 51.7 (S.D. = 11.6) for females.

We found the internal consistency of the Zung to be satisfactory with both samples. Cronbach's alpha was .83 for the clinical sample and .72 for the control sample.

DISCUSSION AND RECOMMENDATIONS

The results of the groups discrimination study have increased our degree of confidence in the use of the Zung Self-Rating Depression Scale as an intake screening instrument with university students. Its internal consistency was satisfactory with both of our samples. The SDS Index successfully discriminated between a control sample of students and students who sought our mental health services. This finding is consistent with previous studies in which clinical samples have produced higher scores than non-clinical samples (Zung, 1965; Zung, Richards, and Short, 1965). This discriminatory power holds for both male and female students in that no significant differences were found between sexes in either sample. These results are consistant with previous evidence that the degree of depression, although not necessarily the incidence, is similar in male and female college students (Oliver and Burkham, 1979; Hammen and Padesky, 1977). A possible explanation is that male and female college students have similar roles, aspirations, and stressors (Oliver and Burkham, 1979).

The finding of significant differences between the clinical and control samples on most of the individual items on the Zung provides support for the manner in which we have used the instrument. As well as attending to the SDS Index, we have noted the scores on individual items and clusters. It is interesting that the two items that did not differentiate the clinical from the control samples involved appetite and weight loss. These items may fail to discriminate in a student population because of the high degree of concern and anxiety about weight, appearance, and eating habits and the widespread frequency of unstable eating patterns, including fad dieting.

Our subjective impressions of the value of the Zung instrument in intake screening reinforce the group discrimination study results. We think it has aided both the efficiency and accuracy with which we have made intake assessments. An additional benefit noted by some therapists is that use of the instrument has relieved them from the detailed and focused interviewing required in assessing depression. Thus, they have been able to concentrate more fully on developing a trusting relationship in their more usual style.

Use of the Zung Self-Rating Depression Scale has made us even more aware of the importance and potential difficulty of assessing depression in a student population. The behavioral cues of depression in students are often quite subtle. Mild depression has been shown to be ten times more frequent than severe depression in this age group (Oliver and Burkham, 1979). Furthermore, depressive episodes are often short-lived in the college population, becoming less acute in two to three weeks in about 50 percent of depressed students (Hammen, 1980). In order to achieve productive and lasting resolution of a crisis it is often important to complete assessment and initiate treatment before cyclic changes or improved circumstances reduce motivation. We conclude that the Zung instrument can assist in this early identification process. Another factor making assessment of depression difficult in student mental health and counseling services is the tendency for older people to minimize the intensity of emotions in adolescents and young adults (Rockwell, Moorman, and Hawkins, 1976).

One concern we entertained when initially including the Zung in our intake procedures was that students might find it intrusive. While an occasional student may leave the instrument blank or complain about the procedure, the vast majority have evidenced no negative reaction to its use. It appears that most students accept the request to fill out the Zung Scale as an appropriate part of their seeking mental health services.

In summary, the Zung Self-Rating Depression Scale has been a helpful addition to our intake procedures. It has enabled us to be more sensitive to the presence of depression in students, both global depression and specific depressive symptoms. Therefore, we recommend experimentation with this instrument to other professionals in student mental health and counseling services.

REFERENCES

1. Beck, A. T., Rush, A. J., Shaw, B. F., and Emery, G.: *Cognitive Therapy of Depression*. New York, Guilford, 1979.
2. Bosse, J. J., Croghan, L. M., and Greenstein, M. B.: Frequency of depression in the freshman year as measured in a random sample by a retrospective version of the Beck Depression Inventory. *Journal of Consulting and Clinical Psychology, 43*:746-747, 1975.
3. Brown, B. M.: Depressed college students and tricyclic antidepressant therapy. *Journal of the American College Health Association, 27*:79-83, 1978.
4. Bumberry, W., McClure, J. N., and Oliver, J. M.: Validation of the Beck Depression Inventory in a university population using psychiatric estimate as the criterion. *Journal of Consulting and Clinical Psychology, 46*:150-155, 1978.
5. Hammen, C. L.: Depression in college students: beyond the Beck Depression Inventory. *Journal of Consulting and Clinical Psychology, 48*:126-128, 1980.
6. Hammen, C. L., and Cochran, S. D.: Cognitive correlates of stress and depression in college students. *Journal of Abnormal Psychology, 90*:23-27, 1981.
7. Hammen, C., and Padesky, C.: Sex differences in the expression of depressive responses on the Beck Depression Inventory. *Journal of Abnormal Psychology, 86*:609-614, 1977.
8. Heinrichs, E. H.: Suicide in the young: demographic data of college-age students in a rural state. *Journal of the American College Health Association, 28*:236-237, 1980.
9. Kraft, P. P.: Suicides during a twenty year period at a state university. *Journal of the American College Health Association, 18*:258-262, 1980.
10. Oliver, J. M., and Burkham, R.: Depression in university students: duration, relation to calendar time, prevalence, and demographic correlates. *Journal of Abnormal Psychology, 88*:667-670, 1979.
11. O'Neil, M. K. and Marziali, E.: Depression in a university clinic population. *Canadian Psychiatric Association Journal, 21*:477-481, 1978.
12. Rockwell, W. J. K., Moorman, J. C., and Hawkins, D.: Individual versus group: outcome in a university mental health service. *Journal of the American College Health Association, 24*:186-190, 1976.
13. Schwartz, A. J., and Reifler, C. B.: Suicide among American colleges and university students from 1970-71 through 1975-76. *Journal of the American College Health Association, 28*:205-210, 1980.
14. Talley, J. E.: Descriptive statistics for counseling and psychological services. Unpublished report, Duke University, 1983.
15. Whitney, W., Cadoret, R. J., and McClure, J. N.: Depressive symptoms and academic performance in college students. *American Journal of Psychiatry, 128*:766-770, 1971.

16. Zung, W. W. K.: A self-rating depression scale. *Archives of General Psychiatry,* *12*:63-70, 1965.
17. Zung, W. W. K., Richards, C. D., and Short, M. J.: Self-rating depression scale in an outpatient clinic. *Archives of General Psychiatry, 13*:508, 1965.

Chapter V.

CONSULTATION IN PSYCHIATRIC EMERGENCIES

JANE CLARK MOORMAN, JOHN R. URBACH,
AND DONALD R. ROSS

Introduction

IT is both customary and appropriate that campus mental health professionals put considerable effort into the prevention of psychiatric emergencies among students through clinical services, consultation, and educational activities within the university community. While "psychiatric emergencies" have been defined in many ways, loss of self-control resulting in impulsive behavior is frequently involved. Most often such patients seen in the emergency room have "reached their limit" because of feelings of hopelessness and desperation due to either immobilizing depression or anxiety or self-destructive impulses. Informed, alert university personnel may well see an emotional storm brewing and be able to preclude a major crisis by providing the student with support and/or a referral for professional treatment. Of course, it is not possible to prevent all emergencies and some students do require hospital emergency room evaluation or treatment. Fairly often, difficult questions arise regarding disposition in these cases. Where relevant personal and situational background information can be acquired and taken into account in making a disposition, it is reasonable to expect more positive outcomes in the long run. Unfortunately, limited understanding of the various aspects of responsibility that different university personnel carry for students often precludes what would otherwise be constructive and helpful communication.

ROLES OF EMERGENCY ROOM PSYCHIATRISTS, UNIVERSITY ADMINISTRATORS AND MENTAL HEALTH STAFF

Confidentiality very quickly becomes a central and complex issue as the different kinds of responsibility that emergency room psychiatrists, university administrators, and campus mental health professionals have for students come into focus. While the emergency psychiatrist's primary responsibility is to protect a patient's well-being and confidentiality, a university dean (or other official) carries institutional responsibility not only for individual students but for the well-being of the campus community at large. For this reason, student affairs deans sometimes feel they both need and have a right to know when a student is experiencing a serious psychiatric disturbance; some do not feel such notification, with or without the student's permission, is a violation of confidentiality in any way, given their quasi *in loco parentis* status, and believe it should be routine. These differing perceptions or definitions of professional and administrative responsibility have, at times, led to unnecessary conflict, misunderstanding, frustration, and less than optimal case dispositions involving students. Often such negative experiences which detract from patient care could have been avoided had all responsible parties had access to and an understanding of guidelines for managing student psychiatric emergencies seen in the hospital emergency room.

While university administrators, generally speaking, seek consultation from mental health professionals concerning students having psychological difficulties far more frequently than the reverse, the emergency room psychiatrist should give careful consideration to the potential wealth of information a dean may be able to provide regarding a student presenting a dispositional dilemma.

With the various responsibilities of these professionals in mind, the roles of campus mental health professionals in student emergencies may be several including the following:

1. consultant to university administrators
2. consultant to the emergency room psychiatrist
3. interpreter of university and hospital policies and procedures that may appear at times to conflict
4. therapist of the student

Obviously, there does exist the potential for conflicting loyalties to the university, the student and the colleague caring for him. When the campus mental health professional is also the student's therapist, these situations require that the former very carefully evaluate each request for consultation in order to determine whether the severity of the student's situation warrants the release of confidential information. In some situations one may consult about a student without needing to divulge the therapeutic relationship by discussing guidelines as to how students presenting such situations are generally handled. More often it is appropriate to acknowledge early in the consultation process one's therapeutic relationship with a student, especially in those cases in which such knowledge would be important in disposition planning. Whenever possible, it is always wise to secure the student's permission to discuss the situation before doing so; however, if the student is unable to give such permission, the therapist should discuss what is necessary to provide adequate protection for all concerned.

There is surprisingly little literature pertaining to this particular kind of consultation. Arnstein (1972) points out the dual role of the college psychiatrist as therapist (to the student) and consultant (to the university administration). As a guideline to simultaneously obtaining information from administrators and protecting the confidentiality of the student, he suggests the use of "tact and common sense." Blaine (1964) also outlines the problem of confidentiality and the therapist's divided loyalties by discussing nine problem cases and how they were handled at the Harvard University Health Services. Again, general guidelines are absent, and no case involved emergency room disposition. Szasz (1967) suggests that the college psychiatrist, in practice, breaks confidentiality whenever he considers it best for the patient, college, or community-at-large to do so. In his view, confidentiality is a fiction.

Curran (1969) attempted a systematic appraisal of confidentiality practices as reflected in the policies of 173 college mental health services that responded to a questionnaire on this topic. Interestingly, only nineteen programs had written policies regarding confidentiality. Twenty-two others reported that they followed the Recommended Standards and Practice of the American College Health Association (1964). In accord with the Standards, the majority of mental health services only notified university administrators of a student's involvement with mental health if hospitalization was required or a suicide attempt had been made. The specific issue of breaking confidentiality for the purpose of obtaining information from administrators regarding the student was not addressed.

At Duke University, campus mental health professionals, psychiatric staff in its medical center, and university deans responsible for student affairs conferred together in developing the following guidelines for use by emergency room psychiatric staff in making decisions regarding Duke students. While far from comprising a definitive framework, they have served to enhance emergency psychiatrists' understanding of university resources, from whom it is sometimes appropriate to seek consultation, and university officials' understanding of the legal and ethical issues involved in disposition of psychiatric emergencies involving students. Of course, sound clinical judgment and the safety and welfare of the individual are of primary importance in making dispositions regarding students as they are for all patients.

LEGAL AND ETHICAL ISSUES

Conflicts about notification and disposition planning for students seen in the emergency room seem to revolve around three general principles: (1) the confidential nature of the psychiatrist-patient relationship; (2) the limitations on that confidentiality when the safety of the patient or others is threatened; and (3) the perceived but amorphous obligation of the university to act *in loco parentis* with respect to its students. For any patient, the first two principles always involve an individualized weighing process by the emergency psychiatrist of the relative risks and benefits of withholding versus disclosing information concerning the patient. With students, the addition of the third principle favors limited disclosure to appropriate campus personnel in some cases. (See the discussion following on what information should be revealed.) While clinical assessment of the student in the emergency room is the exclusive province of the examining physician, administrative decisions related to disposition planning are often best made jointly with campus personnel.

WHEN IS NOTIFICATION APPROPRIATE?

In our experience, students seen in the emergency room seem to fall into three broad groups. One group presents with a spectrum of psychosocial and/or psychiatric problems which, however distressing, do not pose a serious threat to the safety of the student or those in the environment. Such students may simply be seeking a chance to talk openly, brief crisis intervention, or an entree into outpatient psychotherapy. They should be accorded the same standard of privacy as any nonstudent patient, and university personnel should not be contacted. However, it may be important to ascertain from the student whether a minimal support network and a stable living situation are available.

A second group presents clear indications of acute psychiatric distress that has overwhelmed judgment and has led to serious destructive behavior, or threats of such behavior, directed at themselves or others. Students taking significant drug overdoses, making suicidal efforts, assaulting others, overtly threatening to harm themselves or others, etc., would fall into this group. In such situations hospitalization is usually indicated; the appropriate campus personnel and, usually, the student's parents should be notified. Special problems are posed by students requiring hospitalization but refusing to be admitted on a voluntary basis. Involuntary hospitalization raises psychological issues of control and authority that are paramount developmental concerns for late adolescents and young adults. Whenever possible, negotiation of a voluntary admission should be attempted. If involuntary commitment proceedings must be initiated, appropriate campus personnel and, when possible, the student's parents or other family members should be directly involved in the process.

A third group of students represents a "gray zone" both diagnostically and with regard to notification. These students may raise serious concerns for the psychiatrist about their judgment, emotional stability, self-care and safety, yet present no overtly dangerous behavior or ideation at the time of initial evaluation in the emergency room. This category might include students with a "mild" drug or alcohol overdose, accelerating depressions, incapacitating anxiety or psychophysiological symptoms, major social isolation, etc. Frequently the true extent of the student's distress and ability to cope may be impossible to determine in an emergency evaluation. Further, the individual's safety and functional capacity may be highly contingent upon a support system and particular living arrangement on or off campus. Such background information may only be available from university personnel and may be crucial in arranging a workable disposition. Often the immediate crisis will be found to be part of an ongoing, perhaps more ominous, pattern that may be known to campus personnel. In these cases, consultation with university staff is often a necessary and useful action.

WHO SHOULD BE CONSULTED?

University personnel who should be consulted are those able to provide useful information while maintaining a high level of discretion. The university mental health service is frequently the most appropriate resource for initial consultation. In addition, a dean responsible for student affairs is often able to provide important background information.

At Duke University, the Counseling and Psychological Services office (CAPS) is a source of consultation frequently utilized by emergency room psychiatrists. As the primary mental health service for Duke students, CAPS is already familiar with many of the students who present to the emergency room with a psychiatric problem. Again, consent from the student should be obtained. Confidentiality is especially important to a college mental health service because of students' particular concerns about privacy when seeking help (Arnstein, 1972 and Farnsworth, 1966). Consequently, CAPS is not always willing to divulge information, especially if the student does not consent. However, staff members are available to assist in evaluating students in the emergency room or to consult with those doing so. Even in situations where the staff member decides it is not best to divulge specific information regarding the student, the consultation is often quite useful for general information regarding diagnosis and disposition options. Furthermore, CAPS is available for follow-up of students seen in the emergency room.

Two deans at Duke have been designated as the most appropriate campus administrators to be notified: the Assistant Dean for Freshmen and the University Dean for Student Life. These deans were chosen because: (1) they have broad responsibilities for students, especially those living in campus residences, and for intervening when personal or environmental safety is threatened; (2) they exercise functions separate from those charged primarily with academic affairs and thus can provide personal help without jeopardizing the student's academic future; and, (3) they provide a greater measure of experience, discretion, and confidentiality than other personnel can.

Whether to notify the student's parents is another issue that needs to be considered on a case-by-case basis. Consultation with the mental health staff or the appropriate dean may help in reaching a decision about family notification.

WHO SHOULD NOTIFY, AND THE PROBLEM OF CONSENT

Whenever notification of a dean or family member is indicated, the student, if able, should be encouraged to give the notification. If the student is unable to do so, the need for such notification should be discussed with him/her ahead of time; the restricted nature of the disclosure and the distinction between the dean's residential and academic authority should be explained. When contact with the family is indicated, it may be more appropriate for the student's therapist or dean to do so than the emergency psychiatrist.

Whenever possible, the student's permission for notification should be sought. Students may express concerns about privacy from particular friends, faculty, or relatives, that should be considered. However, resistance should not prevent notifying the dean or the parents where the physician has determined that notification is necessary. In counterpoint, the "consent" of the student should not be used to relieve the physician entirely of the general obligation to protect the student from unnecessary or avoidable harm that may result from ill-advised disclosure. It is important that the examining psychiatrist document efforts to secure permission in the chart, identifying the patient's agreement or disagreement, and stating the reasons for which notification is necessary.

WHAT INFORMATION SHOULD BE REVEALED?

The emergency room psychiatrist consulting with a dean should use discretion and tact in revealing information about the student. Generally, disclosure should be limited to what the dean needs to know to protect the safety and well-being of the student and the community. The general nature of the problem, the student's current state, the perceived threats from or to the student or others will usually be sufficient. Highly personal, conflictual or embarrassing details, usually not crucial to disposition planning, should not be divulged. Information should be sought from the therapist or dean regarding present functioning, previous problems, and the feasibility of the student's returning to the current residential environment in an effort to make the best possible disposition.

Case Example

Ms. A., a twenty-three year old female senior undergraduate, presented to the emergency room saying she had taken twenty over-the-counter sleeping tablets (doxylamine succinate) three hours prior to her arrival. She then refused to give any more history or discuss why she took the overdose. Medical evaluation and check with the poison control center established that she was not in any physical danger from her ingestion. When the psychiatry resident on call questioned her about suicidal intent, she only smiled and discussed in intellectualized terms her right to suicide if she so chose. She admitted to feeling depressed "for years." The student refused to give assurances that she was not suicidal. She was offered voluntary admission to the psychiatry inpatient service but refused.

At this point the psychiatric resident needed to decide whether involuntary commitment was in the student's best interests. Ms. A.

refused to give or deny permission for the resident to contact CAPS or her dean. A member of the CAPS staff was consulted from whom it was learned that Ms. A. had seen a counselor there several months earlier and had complained of increasing social isolation. She reported having no close friends and lived alone. Consultation with Ms. A.'s non-academic dean revealed that she had withdrawn from school for a year as a sophomore for "personal reasons." There was no knowledge of any more recent difficulties. Ms. A.'s parents could not be immediately contacted.

Due to the history of progressive social withdrawal, lack of an external support system, and the real suicide potential in this patient, involuntary commitment was initiated. After a month of inpatient treatment with tricyclic antidepressants and psychotherapy, Ms. A. was much improved.

Summary

The guidelines discussed here were developed in an effort to address the issues of the emergency psychiatrist's responsibility to the student-patient, the student's right to confidentiality, and the complex consultative roles of university mental health professionals and administrators in a psychiatric emergency. A careful clinical evaluation of the individual student by the psychiatrist in the emergency room provides data upon which to make decisions regarding treatment and disposition. Consultation with the university mental health staff and/or deans responsible for student life can often be useful and even critical in this process. Consent from the student should be obtained before such contact is made. When the student is unwilling or unable to consent, the psychiatrist needs to proceed on the basis of what appears to be in the best interests of the student. Both long-term (e.g., suicidal behavior) and short-term (e.g., stigmatization) consequences of consulting or not consulting need to be considered. At Duke we have found that an established set of guidelines has proven helpful in several ways. It has improved understanding among all personnel, both psychiatric and administrative, of the complex responsibilities carried by each for student-patients. It has reduced confusion in the emergency room over whether to consult with university personnel and how to do so when appropriate. Last but not least, it has resulted in improved care of student-patients by allowing a more comprehensive review of their needs and the best options for meeting them within the university community.

REFERENCES

1. American College Health Association. Recommended Standards and Practices for a College Health Program, Supplement on Ethical and Professional Relations. *Journal of the American College Health Association, 13*:45-89, 1964.
2. Arnstein, R. L.: College psychiatry and community psychiatry. *Journal of the American College Health Association, 20*:257-261, 1972.
3. Blaine, G. B.: Divided loyalties: The college therapist's responsibility to the student, the university and the parents. *American Journal of Orthopsychiatry, 34*:481-485, 1964.
4. Curran, W. J.: Policies and practices concerning confidentiality in college mental health services in the United States and Canada. *American Journal of Psychiatry, 125*:1520-1530, 1969.
5. Farnsworth, D.: *Psychiatry, Education, and the Young Adult.* Springfield, Il., Charles C Thomas, 1966.
6. Szasz, T. S.: The psychiatrist as double-agent. *Trans-Action, 4*:16-24, 1967.

Chapter VI.

COMMUNICATIONS WITH PARENTS

W. J. KENNETH ROCKWELL

Introduction

COMMUNICATING with the parents of emotionally dis-turbed university students is a relatively infrequent activity of students' therapists, but when such communication occurs, the relationship engendered between parents and therapist becomes critically important to the treatment of the student. My purpose is twofold: (1) to discuss some attitudes that may come into play and be influential when parents and therapists are trying to communicate with one another about a disturbed student; and (2) to discuss some specific situations in which parents and a therapist encounter one another and possible concerns and responses of both. There is not space to present alternative ways in which a therapist might deal with the various situations to be outlined, so only one method of management will be given. The observations are made presupposing a setting in which parents are encountered usually without prior relationship with the therapist and usually due to circumstances of tension or crisis in which contact with them will be brief and at most sporadic. In any event, when communicating with parents the therapist's guiding objective is to form an alliance designed to promote the growth and development of the student.

Literature Review

The literature is sparse. Blaine and McArthur (1961) recounted some of the issues that must be dealt with when contacting parents in emergency situations in which hospitalization of a student is necessary. They advocated parental consultation and approval prior to hospitalization. This is not always practical. Trossman (1968) delineated various situations in which a mental health service and parents came in contact. The majority of students coming to his service lived at home. He described the students' problems with parents from a developmental frame of reference and differentiated conflicts which required no parental involvement with students' treatment from those which indicated a few sessions with parents or a recommendation for family treatment. The emphasis was on family dynamics rather than management problems per se, and the parental ambience was presumed to be pathogenic. There are scattered comments elsewhere relevant to parent participation in student treatment, usually made with reference to a case history.

GENERAL CONSIDERATIONS

Attitudes of Therapists Toward Parents

My impression is that the average expectable attitude of university student therapists toward parents falls somewhere between: "Parents are a nuisance to be dealt with and dismissed as expeditiously as possible," and, "Parents, being the causal agents in the student's problem to begin with, are to be excluded at all costs from my corrective relationship with their child." Such attitudes are unproductive. Among their numerous origins are more than a generation of official teaching that has distorted the meaning of separation of the late adolescent from family of origin and misconstrued the means of effecting it.

Where therapist anti-parental bias exists, it needs to be identified and at least controlled for, if not resolved. This is axiomatic if the therapist is to collaborate with parents successfully, but in a more subtle way it is just as true if therapy is to be optimum, even when there is no contact with parents. Among the many reasons why therapist anti-parental bias is unuseful, one is a standout: blood is thicker than therapy. Any therapist who vies seriously with parents for the loyalty of a student will, in all probability, find himself without a patient, regardless of whether this is done psychologically in the "therapy" per se, or in confrontation involving the parents directly. Parental control of students via purse strings is the reason most often cited by therapists and students. Psychological reasons are more pervasive and potent. On the average, students are far more identified with their parents than they are aware of, much less admit to. Where loyalty is not even particularly an issue, overtly or covertly derogating parents assaults the student in two ways: (1) some aspects of the characteristics being derided have usually been incorporated by the student; and (2) the possibility of genetic influence, including psychological characteristics, is in the public consciousness, students included.

The concept of "the identified patient" has perhaps served to moderate anti-parental bias. Using this concept, it will be assumed that the student is the identified patient and the rest of the family are unidentified patients. This may be so, and often enough parents have identified themselves as patients elsewhere, but a student's therapist should not approach the parents as such directly as it is out of context and will only serve to distort communications and alienate parents. Regardless of what he has heard about the parents from the student, the therapist's proper approach is one that conveys the expectation that they will be a positive force in the collaborative effort to promote resolution of the emotional problem and forward progress in the student's development. In other words, the therapist keeps to himself his speculations about or observations of potential parental pathological influences, and speaks only to the healthy side of their egos which he can assume is operating for the well-being of their child. Few parents are so enmeshed in their own problems that they cannot respond to this approach with at least an effort to exert a positive influence on their child's situation.

Attitudes of Parents Toward Emotionally Disturbed Students, Treatment, and Therapists

Assuming that parents have just been apprised that their child is in emotional difficulty, the announcement will "turn on" virtually simultaneously all of the following concerns, and more. These concerns, embedded in alarm, constitute the mental set with which the therapist will be dealing, and perhaps the questions from parents will come somewhat in the following order:

1. How serious is it?
2. What kind of difficulty?
3. Is he suicidal? (Few will think in terms of danger to others, and if this is the case, the shock will be tremendous.)
4. Need for hospitalization? If so, how long?
5. What are the immediate implications: Does this mean he will have to leave school? If so, will he ever return? Would the school have him back? Can't he be treated and at least finish this semester?
6. Future implications: Does this mean chronic mental illness?
7. What do we need to do now: Come down, have him come home, call often?
8. How do we relate to him now? Which may imply: What have we done wrong (clashes with child or lack of relationship, parental fighting, differences in child rearing practices, interparental differences in other attitudes)?

And immediate background concerns, less often directly expressed:

9. Loss of control/influence over child's situation.
10. Adjustments and disruptions in parents' plans for semester or longer.
11. Expense: Of treatment; of dropping out of school if this is to be the case.

After being overwhelmed by a telephone introduction to a situation they only half believe exists, most parents will focus their attention on what is being done now. No list can be compiled of all the predictable fantasies a parent might have about treatment of emotional disturbances or about those who do it. Except in instances in which the child or some other family member has undergone sustained and successful treatment, the following general attitudes are predictable however: skepticism and misunderstanding of what the therapist is relating and a charge of negativity toward the bearer of bad news. This last reaction is primitive and "unacceptable" as such, but is ubiquitous and varies only in degree. Occasionally it is acknowledged. More often such personalized negativity toward an unknown party is bewildering to the parents and to the therapist if he is not prepared for it. The amount of time it takes parents to adjust themselves to their child's status will depend in large part on their previous level of awareness of it. If their alarm decreases, their belief that their child is in difficulty and their ability to assimilate information about it will increase, and their negativity toward the bearer of bad news will decrease.

Attitudes of Students Toward
Parent-Therapist Communications

On the average students probably have fewer concerns about seeing a therapist or their parents knowing of it than parents have about therapists and vice versa. Witness the number of students who tell their parents that they are being seen. But for some students it signifies that they "couldn't make it on their own" or they think (or know) that their parents will see it as a stigma. Questions of loyalty also become involved. For the less independent it is a question of what family secrets have been shared with the therapist and whether the family would see this as betrayal; for the more independent it is a question of which personal matters shared with the therapist does the family need to know about. Most students' attitudes about parent-therapist interactions will be determined by the nature of the interactions rather than by any preconceived ideas.

Confidentiality

Confidentiality exists to protect the interests of patients. It is not a divine right of therapists, but it is a useful tool in treatment. The therapist must know the state law on privileged communications governing his discipline, and policies on same of organizations he represents. In the mélange of gray areas uncovered by laws and policies, good common sense, good professional judgment, and maintaining the best interest of the patient will suffice except in precedent setting cases. A rigid approach to confidentiality will tend to obstruct therapist-parent communications and this is not good for alliances. For example, when a call from a parent starts with, "Have you talked with my son, X?" the response should be in any case, "I can neither affirm nor deny this." Assuming the case in which the therapist has seen the student, and parents rarely ask that question when the therapist has not, a "Yes" response is an unnecessary breach of confidentiality and a "No" response will amost inevitably be followed by detail from the parent which makes it plain that only the student could have divulged the information. Being caught barefaced is an inferior way of commencing constructive dialogue. If the therapist's non-committal response does not bring on parental commentary, the former can follow up with a request for information and questions that may be pursued. The parent can give many particulars which can inform the therapist about both student and family, and the therapist can talk in generalities, including the need for proper authorization to communicate and the reasons therefore, in such a way as to lay the foundation for further communication. Parents are usually calling when the student is in crisis, in many cases of which the therapist would have been calling the parents in a matter of days, and in some of those cases without authorization.

Parental Control

Parental control is a major issue being continuously addressed covertly or overtly in the communications and negotiations between therapists and parents. It requires a full scale evaluation and many hours of therapy over time during which the control issue is made overt and its ramifications are reviewed in various contexts in order to deal with this one matter adequately. Such an undertaking requires the consent, cooperation, and participation of the parents. University students' therapists are seldom involved with parents over a sufficient period of time to negotiate for, conduct, or even recommend family systems therapy when there might be indications for it. In the brief and sporadic encounters that they usually do have, therapists' management of control issues is one of the major determinants in whether or not a productive alliance with the parents will occur. During initial encounters the therapist must not threaten or challenge the parents' sense of control over their child (from their standpoint the student has usually done more than enough of this already), but rather seek ways to reinforce their sense of control over their own feelings and behavior. Effecting this subtle shift of focus may be a difficult maneuver. Sometimes the therapist can promote the alliance by pointing out the limitations of his own role and armamentarium and, while avoiding conveying a sense of anyone's powerlessness, suggest the importance of finding ways in which everyone can pull in the same direction.

EXAMPLE SITUATIONS

Crisis 1. Announcing and Discussing Hospitalization

Parents should be involved in the decision to hospitalize single students whenever this is possible. Often it is not, so in the following discussion it is assumed that the student has been hospitalized and the therapist is his primary physician in the hospital. Some issues are similar if the parents are being brought into the decision to hospitalize or if the therapist has been involved in the hospitalization, turns the student over to a physician, and is speaking with the parents later.

Purpose of the First Contact

Therapists become accustomed quickly to severely out of control students. Parents usually are not and the impact on the latter of their child being hospitalized cannot be overestimated. The first call has the dual purpose of imparting information and assisting parents in keeping their anxiety within controllable limits. To the extent to which it can be achieved, the latter is accomplished by helping the parents focus on what they are going to do and this involves telling them what is already being done and giving them what other basic information is available from which to plan a course of action. The best single measure of a future successful collaboration with parents is their ability to cope with uncertainty, as measured by relatively low levels of demand for more information and explanation than is possible in a new and evolving situation.

When and Whom to Contact

It is preferable to have the student's cooperation before making the first contact. Many students "don't want (their) parents to know" and refuse to give permission, which is unrealistic except in the few cases in which it is known that the student is totally out of contact with parents anyway. Twelve hours is about the practical limit of non-notification beyond which the probabilities begin to rise steeply that further delay will constitute an unproductive obstruction of the parents' need to do their parenting and hinder the formation of a constructive parent-therapist alliance. In the course of this time period, however, a number of students who initially refused to give permission will acquiesce. Some students wish to make the first call home themselves and this is usually appropriate for those who need that type of control. Such calls should be followed at once by one from the physician. It is preferable when both parents can be reached simultaneously, but the more usual course of events, which the therapist should foresee and plan for, is that one parent is reached during the day and the other or both will want contact in the evening. Occasionally a student will make a sharp distinction as to parent of choice to be contacted.

Initial Exchanges

The sequence is usually as follows: announcement of the hospitalization and immediate circumstances surrounding it; comprehension-seeking response by parent, more or less stunned; further elaboration of circumstances by therapist; ventilation of concerns by parent intermixed with responses to these by therapist; turn of focus to sequence of immediate actions parent will take.

After identifying himself fully, and then the parent, the therapist announces the hospitalization and its location and then quickly comments on the physical status of the student. (1) In the event of physical harm or danger, such as after a suicide attempt, this fact must be disclosed along with the student's current condition and the measures being taken to improve it. At this juncture, details of how to get to the hospital (and the Intensive Care Unit if the student is being treated there) and what doctor to contact will be more important to the parents than background details as to what brought about the attempt. (2) In the more usual case, after the therapist makes clear the absence of physical danger, he introduces the rationale for hospitalization in general terms with such phrases as "sufficiently emotionally distubed," and the "need to be where he can settle down while we are evaluating him further." By this time the parent is usually asking questions to which the therapist responds, during which he asks about the parents' awareness of any upset in their child. If they have been aware, as is more usual, then the hospitalization can frequently be made more comprehensible to them by connecting what the therapist knows about the sequence of events with what they know. The student's current status and management are also more comprehensible when fitted into this framework.

If the parents have not been aware of any disturbance, then the therapist has the more difficult task of making comprehensible both the issue of emotional disturbance and the necessity for hospitalization. The situation is made even more difficult since the therapist is always trying to avoid transmitting embarrassing content not already known to the parents. Under these conditions the therapist can be concrete about and emphasize the overt symptoms and behaviors which led to the hospitalization and can properly defer an explanation of why the situation arose until later when more information is available. The intensity of the situation will lead to an increased tendency on the part of the therapist to try to reduce parental anxiety by giving more and more detail and explanation about the student's past and present state of mind. Such information usually just leads to more parental speculation, questions, and anxiety. Unless the student's life is in serious danger at this point or there is a threat of brain damage, a more reassuring therapeutic posture is to suggest that the student himself will probably be able to throw more light on the situation in due course.

The therapist would like to be able to describe a situation serious enough to require hospitalization without being alarming. This is impossible, of course. To attempt to mitigate the alarm, the therapist tries to convey the perspective that the situation is serious but manageable and that its critical aspects are time-limited. If suicidal ideation is a major feature or the primary reason for the hospitalization, this must be addressed in the initial contact. Parents need time to process this information; it will come out sooner or later, and "shielding" them will only imply that they are not thought capable of dealing with it, an implication that will undermine their self-confidence. If suicidal ideation has occurred but is a secondary feature in the disturbance, mention of it can be deferred, unless a parent inquires directly. The therapist's hope is that the student will be able to incorporate this piece of content in context as he talks over his condition with his parents later.

Special Issues

1. "Who made the decision to hospitalize?" The need for hospitalization is a medical judgment, of course, but the act is a decision in which the student does not participate if he is committed, does participate if he is not. In the former case the circumstances should be overwhelming enough to help convince the parents that the proper thing has been done. In the latter case, after outlining the reasons on which the medical judgment was based, it is important to introduce into the account the student's participation in the decision. This can include comments on the student's good sense in seeking help, evaluating his own situation, and accepting medical opinion. This will help to alleviate parental anxiety that something has been done to their child or that he has lost his mind. It will usually help the credibility (in the eyes of the parents) of both the therapist and student if they are seen as having collaborated in the hospitalization. Parental anxiety is often further reduced when the reversible nature of the procedure is pointed out with the reassurance that the vast majority of such hospitalizations are relatively brief. At this point it can usually also be pointed out that when the parents have had time to talk with their child and acquire further information, they will most certainly be participating in the decision to discharge.

2. "We want a second opinion" about either the need for hospitalization or the treatment. During initial communications this represents, mostly, parental groping for control over the situation rather than an attack on the unknown physician (*vide* the ubiquitous negative reaction, however). The best response to this request or demand is immediate agreement followed by an attempt to make some sort of personal connection between the parents and a local psychiatrist. Even a circuitous connection helps. For example, their family doctor is acquainted with a physician in the vicinity of the university and the latter recommends a psychiatrist. Suggesting the search usually enhances the therapist's standing with the parents; and if a physician is found with whom they feel some connection, their anxiety will be reduced.

3. "Was he using drugs?" Whether he has received general authorization from the student to speak with the parents or not, this is one

question the response to which the therapist will want to have discussed in advance with the student, if at all possible. The therapist is in the best position if the student gives him a "free hand," as a number of factors are at issue. Parents in general are properly aware that a substantial amount of experimentation with drugs (alcohol included) takes place on campuses, and they are more aware than are their children of the general level of association between drug use and emotional and behavioral disorders, so the question is a natural one. If it can be answered with a flat "No," a great deal of inappropriately based anxiety can be alleviated (although everyone may later on wish the hospitalization had resulted from a state of temporary intoxication). If the answer is "Yes," meaning acute toxicity, the usually brief nature of the immediate state can be pointed out. Chronic drug abuse will always be a factor in management and planning for the student, even if it is not the primary cause of hospitalization, so it might as well be addressed and put into context when the question is asked. When drug use or abuse has occurred, parents almost always find out about it, usually from their child, and soon. Better that they should receive accurate information in a balanced discussion from the therapist, for if the latter withholds, the damage is immense to his credibility and that of future therapists. If the student tells the therapist not to discuss drug use, the best that the therapist can do is to refer the parents to the student for comment. Even under the stress of their child's being hospitalized, most parents are able without excessive anxiety to defer discussion of many content areas other than drugs until they can talk with their child directly.

4. "What is the diagnosis?" At the time of initial communications the diagnosis has often not been firmly fixed, but in any event the therapist must first find out what the parents mean by the question. If the question is fundamental and means "Do you have a guidepost to treatment?" the response can almost always be affirmative, even if it is most preliminary, and it can be dealt with in symptomatic rather than diagnostic terms. If the parents mean a final diagnosis in technical terms with prognostic import, the therapist will not have an evaluation sufficient to provide that information at this point, but needs to pursue the implications of the question in terms of the anxieties it represents that may be based on a great deal of relevant observation of the student, family history, or even prior evaluation.

Crisis 2. Dropping Out of School

Dropping out of school occurs under a variety of circumstances and parents are often not involved beforehand in this decision. In the following example the circumstances are such that the student had decided to drop out and the Dean has agreed. The parents have arrived to pick their child up, but one or both of them want him to stay in school. The therapist has not seen the student before, but he is called upon ostensibly to clarify emotional issues concommitant with the withdrawal (whether or not the dropout is for personal or medical reasons) and often, covertly, to buttress the position of the party seeking the consultation. The therapist needs to proceed as follows.

Obtain Information from the Dean

Ask about the circumstances surrounding the withdrawal, including the type of withdrawal and need for medical clearance for return, if any.

See the Student First

Find out: what the student wants from the therapist, why he is withdrawing, how he fits withdrawing into his long range plans, what he plans to do during the period of dropout, plans for returning to school; attitude toward school in general and this school in particular; attitude toward parents; need for treatment (level of anxiety/depression, including any suicidal thoughts; diagnosis). The student may need to be reassured in regard to returning to school.

See the Parents

When student and therapist have never met before this occasion, it is important for the latter to remember that his credibility with the parents will be virtually nil. Therefore one of the first questions the therapist should ask the parents is how the evaluation fits into their overall picture of the situation and what weight would they attach to anything that the therapist said, given that they do not know him and he does not know their child.

The response should give the therapist some assessment of parental willingness to listen and how much they can hear. He is trying to help the parents become supportive of a decision that has already been made with little or no input from them and is one that they do not like. Ultimately the therapist may be able to put this specific situation in some perspective through the generalization that a large percentage of graduates have withdrawn at some point within their academic careers, but one way of avoiding an immediate confrontation over the therapist's lack of credibility can sometimes be to say to the parents, "You know your child better than I do; I need your assessment of him in order to make any sort of evaluation." This should help to bring them into the proceedings and hence give them a feeling of greater control; make them feel that their views are valued; open the door to collaboration as opposed to adversary relationships; help the therapist learn some things about the child and the parents which may shape the evaluation and recommendations; and may lead everyone out of a side-taking situation, in which the major effort by each parent will be to get the therapist to support his or her position with the idea that whosoever gets the upper hand will then be able to persuade the child. The therapist, then, is attempting to refocus the parents' attention on the need for further assessment for their child in a transitional situation, and draw them away from already fixed conclusions and/or power struggles.

In the evaluation the therapist is looking for (1) the parents' relationship with one another and with their child; (2) their evaluation of their child's maturity level; (3) their aspirations of their child; (4) their supportiveness; (5) how much control they are willing to give their child.

The direction in which the therapist is attempting to get the parents to move is toward: (1) getting them to put their child's behavior in a decision-making context, as opposed to "impulse" or "failure," or purely "illness-behavior," and (2) getting them to support the child's present decision (or indecision) and not becoming involved in a power struggle wtih or "take over" for the child whom they may see as having proven himself to be "incompetent" by not being able or willing to stay in school, progress on schedule, and so forth. If the therapist senses that the parents have some capacity to relinquish power struggles at this point and become supportive of the student, questions may be pursued along the following lines. Even if they see it as a "wrong" decision; how willing are they to let their child make wrong decisions? When asked this question, parents will often say they are quite willing to let their child make wrong decisions, but "this one is different." Indeed, it is different in the sense of magnitude, so what are their limits on the decisions that they will allow their child to make? For example, if he can't drop out of school, was going to school his decision in the first place?

After all this preliminary work, i.e., student and parent evaluation, the therapist will be expected by the parents to give an option. Hopefully by then his opined sense of the situation will be a reinforcement of the sense that the parents by now have arrived at, namely, that their child has made the decision to leave and it is now a matter of how best to support that decision and proceed from there, that is, make plans for the immediate future, such as the amount of time "sitting around home," activity level, need for supervision, how to respond to (the child), treatment, interim job, interim schooling; then, reentry process. It is well to discuss the last issue with parents at this point in order to reassure them that return to school is possible from the standpoint of the university administration. It may or may not be appropriate to discuss the issue with the student at this time and therefore this should be gone over with the parents prior to the session with all together.

Meet With Student and Parents Together

In this family session the therapist is attempting to get the parents and student moving in the same direction or in any event to get communication going between them with that in view. Therefore, this interview involves getting parents and student to plan their next moves together. At this time the therapist can answer questions about treatment and about type of medical clearance, if any, that will be needed prior to returning to school. Reassurance about reentry into school can be given once again if the student seems in need of it.

Crisis 3. Parents Call Therapist About Student in Crisis

Often parents will call a therapist about their child whom they feel to be in crisis and want to know what the therapist is doing or what they themselves should do, and the therapist has no authorization to communicate. In this situation the therapist must attempt to be the least obstructive about communications as possible since diminished communications will only increase parental anxiety, which will not help the student and thereby defeat the aims of both parents and therapist. Also, the therapist does not wish to alienate parents whom. he may be calling shortly about their child's being hospitalized or his need for being taken home or otherwise supported. After the "neither affirm nor deny" response (see Confidentiality above) the therapist can immediately reassure the parents that he wants to talk with them and to help them with their child and then the therapist can ask the parents to tell him what they know about the situation. Often this is a great deal, but even when it is not, the therapist can then advise them on what he thinks they should do next on the basis of what they have told him, saying that this is his usual advice in a situation such as they have described. The therapist's advice may be slanted by what he knows of the student personally, but it can be left to parental conjecture as to whether or not this is so. Actually, the therapist's advice can be very directive at times, such as: "From what you have told me, I think you should stay at home and await developments"; "I think you should come down immediately"; "I would call X and try to get his authorization to speak with his therapist"; "I would call Dean X who might know something about this situation." Also, the therapist can comment as to what appears to be the dangerousness of the situation, if any. This serves to elicit the parents' feelings about that issue, lets them know that the therapist is also evaluating it, and gives them a "professional opinion" based on the information that has been adduced up to that point. The therapist can describe his own credentials and experience, the university's concern for students in difficulty and machinery for dealing with it, local facilities where professional help may be obtained, and the concern that fellow students have for those in trouble. He may even suggest that if the parents know a roommate or friend that they try to contact such people, and the therapist may help to locate such students or attempt to have them contact the parents. In short the therapist can open up communication with himself and attempt to get the parents to establish communication with others so that they will feel more in touch with the situation, all without any breach of confidentiality.

Crisis 4. Therapists and Uncooperative Parents

Therapists are, rarely, in the peculiar position of calling parents with or without authorization, identifying themselves, requesting that the parents do something for their child, and then having the parents refuse. This has been known to occur, even when the child has been hinting about suicide to the parents. Under such circumstances the parents may have had the feeling that the child was "crying wolf" again and they may have been correct in this assessment, but the responsibility for making such a judgment must be put squarely on them. When parents fail to respond to a request by the therapist the first thing for the therapist to do is to locate, if possible, anyone who might have a relationship with the parents, go over the situation with that person, and request them to beseech the parents to take some action. In a situation of any dangerousness, the appropriate dean should be notified. Finally, the therapist should document for his own records the nature of the situation, the various communications he made with respect to it, and the results of those communications.

Crisis 5. Announcing Death by Suicide

It is usually not the function of the Mental Health Service to be first in the university community to notify parents of death by suicide. This is just as well as suicide has stigma enough attached to it already, and to have someone from the Mental Health Service calling would imply that the student had been seen there, potentially another stigma. When the stunned parents begin to sift through the background of the suicidal situation, however, the question will usually arise as to whether their child had seen some person on campus who deals with emotional disturbances, be it a professor or psychiatrist. There is no more delicate situation and it is an occasion for which the mental health professional should have all the relevent laws and local policies already fixed in his head. If the student has been seen professionally and unless the law expressly forbids disclosure from the records of the deceased, the humane course is to attempt to provide the parents with information which will help satisfy their need to know what happened. (If the student has not been seen professionally, university therapists should not be involved in direct discussion with parents.) The basic questions that parents will be asking themselves and others in this situatin may be obvious, but are probably worth repeating: (1) Why did he do it? in the immediate sense of now; (2) Why did he do it? in the long range sense of looking for repeated patterns and tendencies; (3) How could hope fail in someone of such promise? (4) What could I have done to prevent it? (5) What could others have done to prevent it? (6) What did I do wrong to contribute to or cause it? and, (7) What did others do wrong to contribute to or cause it? But these questions are being asked in multiple senses ranging from the strictly behavioral to the philosophical.

The basic task of the therapist at this time is to make the dead student appear in as favorable a light as possible and identify, underscore, and support parental strengths, which they will need in the months and years ahead as they attempt to manage their grief and work through their relationship with their child. It is the time when the therapist must be most conscious of his basic attitudes toward all parents and toward these parents in particular. The therapist must try to build into his reponses to the direct questions of the parents an affirmative response to their unasked question: "Will we be able to control our own feelings, particularly the tendency to attack ourselves or others?" His opportunity to evaluate the parents' capabilities in this regard and to provide them with a forum for demonstrating their capabilities will most likely come in the review with the parents of his contact with and management of the student. If the therapist is self-exonerative or self-critical, he creates an atmosphere which will heighten parental turmoil. If he is open, mildly self-evaluative, and controlled, the parents are more likely to see this as a reflection of their own capabilities, or at least it presents them with a model to which they can refer later in their own working-through processes. Also, in his discussion of management the therapist is in a particularly good position to become an ally of the parents if he is able to say he encouraged the student to communicate with them.

One of the basic dichotomies in attitudes toward suicide is as follows: suicide occurs only when an individual is overwhelmed by impulse and no rational judgment is involved; and, rational and irrational forces are involved, their balance dependent on the circumstances. Simply put, some parents would prefer that their child's suicide be a rational decision; others that it be due to forces beyond the child's control. In later stages of their analysis of most suicides parents will be left with unanswered questions and will come to recognize insoluble ambiguity in the matter of balance between rational and irrational forces. At the time of the interview(s) under consideration here a therapist will be of more help if he can determine the parents' present position on this issue and shape his responses to accord more with what they believe at the moment. It is not the function of the therapist to raise challenges to parental belief systems at this point and he should avoid expositions of his own beliefs, even when seemingly invited to give them, because of the inevitable conflicts that will arise. The therapist should limit his revelations about the student to information about overt symptoms and behaviors, and embarrassing content should be avoided if at all possible. He should absolutely avoid complicated psychodynamic formulations and explanations. Parents will need more distance in time from the event and more time in extent to mull over complex psychology, if they ever want to, and anything presented quickly or as a neat explanation will ultimately be viewed as "cheap" and demeaning.

Non-Crisis

Contacts are less frequent with parents of students who are not in medical and/or academic crisis. They occur under conditions of less stress for all and so tend to be less problematic, but not necessarily so.

Non-Crisis 1. Arranging for Treatment

Occasionally parents will contact the therapist and/or bring the student to get the latter established in treatment, often as a follow up to treatment in or out of a hospital. This can be a good occasion for the therapist to establish a relationship with the parents as well as to obtain a history from them during which their relationship with their child can be explored. Also, the therapist can find out about their expectations of treatment and try to rectify misconceptions they may have about what treatment can do and/or what the therapist expects to be doing in treatment. Comments such as "we only want the best" and "we have heard such good things about you" call for particularly vigorous discussion of parental expectations about treatment. Parental expectations as to future communications should be established and it is well to have from the student full authorization for communications in advance in a situation that has a higher than average probability of proceeding to crisis. Finally, financial responsibility and limitations can be established.

When parents are making arrangements for a student's treatment, they often have definite opinions about which discipline they want. The student's feelings should be sought, of course, but if there is no manifest conflict, the parents' wishes should be acceded to without further comment and an offer made to help them find a therapist of their preferred persuasion if they are not already talking to one. The aim is to promote the parents' support of treatment and this is not best done at this point by challenging their choice or educating them as to differences among the disciplines. If a preferred discipline is simply inaccessible, all one can do is review the available resouces. If the parents ask the therapist's opinion about what discipline or therapeutic persuasion would be appropriate to the situation, then the therapist is invited into the role of educator and should speak freely, while acknowledging his bias and his preliminary and limited knowledge of the student's clinical status. The therapist can offer a brief description of his treatment armamentraium and a modest opinion of his judgment as to when and when not to use his various tools. If, after discussion, the parents or the student seem to be uneasy about the therapist's approach, the therapist can best serve by participating in the search for a closer match with parental or student wishes.

Once they have settled upon a given therapist to treat their child, parents will sometimes say, "We are putting you in charge." This is often said by parents who live far away or whose own activities make them literally unavailable for periods of time, but the therapist needs to check out in some detail just what he is being put in charge of. The aim is to limit his charge to therapy and to eliminate other responsibilities, but even this can be deceptive, because there is no way to define precisely the role of the therapist. What the therapist needs to achieve, most basically, is the position in which it is agreed that it will be left to his judgment as to what to communicate to the parents and when to communicate it. The therapist should understand that they do not mean "everything," and provide them with some ready examples that will at least give them pause for reflection, such as hospitalization. This is the decision in which the therapist will be most influential. Do the parents want to know absolutely in advance of the fact? What about an emergency? Then the therapist must give them some of his criteria for an emergency. What about dropping out of school or a medical leave of absence? When do they want to be brought into this: As soon as it is brought up in therapy, before any final decision is made, afterwards? What about changes in career direction or major? When do they want to be brought into these decisions? What about major life incidents, not necessarily affecting administrative status, such as being raped or shot at? When do they want to know about such, if ever? The responses to these situations will not provide for all contingencies, but they should help to give everyone a better understanding of how much the parents are willing to rely on the judgment of the child, how much on the therapist, and at what point they are going to want to be brought in on any decision making. The responses will give a baseline to which the therapist can refer in deciding when he is expected to communicate with the parents. There are times when it may be useful to get a signed agreement in writing.

Non-Crisis 2. Entering a Treatment in Progress

When parents enter the picture for the first time in a treatment that is already underway, establishing and maintaining orderly and productive communication with them may be more complicated than it is when they are involved from the beginning of a student's treatment, but not necessarily so. The therapist needs to do a few things in the following order.

1. Learn the reason for the communication *now*. It may not be problematic. The parents may be calling to let the therapist know they have become aware that their child is in treatment and that they, the parents, are supportive of it. The parents may also wish to know if the therapist wants information or may want to give the therapist information. The major, or minor, purpose of the call may be to evaluate the therapist. The therapist can give his credentials and experience without breaching any confidences. Parental approval of the therapist, a second opinion of the therapist as it were, can be very reassuring to the student. In the most unproblematic instances, the parents merely want to open up the line of communication if needed, and make themselves available.

2. If the parents want information about the student or about the treatment, the situation becomes more problematic and the first step is to secure from the student an authorization for communication. At this time the therapist can learn from the student the latter's view of why the parents are becoming involved at this point and how the

student feels about it.

3. Assuming that authorization is granted, the therapist can then take up with the parents their questions about their child's condition, the need for treatment, what treatment is being given, and other issues of their concern (see General Considerations).

4. If the therapist is contacted directly by the parents or if the desire for such contact is communicated through the student and the student does not grant authorization (and the therapist should give the reasons for this denial a very thorough review) the therapist should send the parents a letter, which has been reviewed with the student, stating simply that he has no authorization to communicate with them. He will do well to include in the letter an expression of his desire in general to communicate with parents but explaining that there are times in students' lives, usually of relatively short duration, when they want to exclude parents from their problem solving efforts.

Non-Crisis 3. Mail

Communications by mail are less frequent than by phone or in person. There is not space to describe the many contingencies which prompt letters from parents, but fortunately, the medium implies less urgent need to respond. All letters should be acknowledged and the basic message conveyed by the therapist should be one of a desire for open communications, but the form of the acknowledgment will depend on student authorization or lack of it. The problem with communicating in writing beyond acknowledgment is basically that there is no way for a letter to provide its own context. Only a document of novel length could begin to do this. Therefore, a letter will inevitably be taken out of context, raising more questions than it settles. In any event a written response should be reviewed with the student and revised if necessary prior to being sent.

Conclusion

In order to collaborate with parents properly, the need for a great amount of time should be clear by now. If the mental set of the therapist is that parents are at best a distraction, little time will be given them, and that grudgingly. The tension thus generated will undermine treatment of the student.

Whether the encounter with parents is unscheduled due to crisis, as in the majority, or scheduled at the convenience of the therapist, the latter needs to make time available. Experience will show that it takes more time than therapists expect, for example, thirty minutes for a "5 minute" phone call, three hours for a one hour office session. (These requirements become reduced, of course, with repeated contacts over an extended period with the same parents.) A "plenty of time" approach relieves both therapist and parents of much pressure immediately and allows them to arrive in relatively orderly fashion at the conclusion that not all the problems at issue can be resolved at once but that they have had a thorough review, that plans are in place, and that therapist and parents have established some common vocabulary for use in future communications.

REFERENCES

1. Blaine, G. B., and McArthur, C. C.: *Emotional Problems of the Student.* Garden City, Doubleday, 1961, p. 133ff.
2. Trossman, B.: The role of parents in a student mental health clinic. *J of the American College Health Association, 16*(3):248-252, 1968.

Chapter VII.

STAFF RETREATS

CHRISTINE D. BELL, JANE CLARK MOORMAN,
AND ELINOR T. ROY

THERE is often resistance to the idea of attending a retreat with one's co-workers. To some, the word "retreat" has negative connotations: the troops falling back, a bunch of religious fanatics meditating in a cave, or a "touchy-feely" encounter group. Our definition of a retreat does not encompass sensitivity training, but, rather, focuses on a goal-directed team building effort, concentrating on group tasks and the celebration of achievements. Our experience has shown that an organization stands to gain a great deal in effectiveness and productivity through staff retreats. That the organization can, in fact, advance through such retreats.

From August of 1980 until January of 1982, staff members at Counseling and Psychological Services (CAPS) of Duke University held four retreats. Staff members found them to be beneficial to the organization, to themselves, and thus, to the students served. It is proposed here that such retreats might prove useful to similar organizations. These retreats increased staff participation in organizational goal-setting and planning, improved performance, strengthened group cohesion, enhanced cooperation among professionals of various disciplines, and helped to prevent "burnout." This chapter suggests a theoretical framework for retreats, describes a design for retreats, and discusses some of the specific gains made by the CAPS organization as a result of retreats.

ORGANIZATIONAL DEVELOPMENT THEORY AND STAFF RETREATS

The professional literature yielded little direct theoretical support for holding staff retreats for college counseling and mental health professionals. It did, however, describe retreats that were held for businesses, primarily by means of the organizational development intervention known as team building. This team building approach, as suggested by organizational development theory, provides the theoretical foundation for conducting staff retreats.

French and Bell (1978) define organizational development as "A long-range effort to improve an organization's operating effectiveness and renewal processes." Organizational development is based on the theory that long-range opportunities for individual growth within the organization are important, and that the effective management of change is essential in the process of the organization's growth. An organizational development intervention is defined here as "the structured activities designed to move an organization from 'where it is' to 'where it wants to be,' " and the team building effort in particular serves to provide a "wide variety of diverse activities designed to improve a team's effectiveness as a unit . . . (that) may relate to ways to perform the task better or ways to improve relations between team members" (French and Bell, 1978).

A retreat, as a means of team building, not only allows the organization to improve its group-directed efforts, but it also provides an environment in which individuals who normally work apart from one another and who are naturally divided by the realms of their particular professional biases and individual personalities can learn to relax together and to gain a new perspective on their work. Retreats also increase the participants' trust of one another, and prevent individual as well as organizational burnout. A retreat is a special type of meeting held in a pleasant setting, away from the office in order to avoid mundane distractions, and it is structured in a manner that allows people to make long-range plans for both themselves professionally and the organization, to relax, and to enjoy themselves.

PLANNING A RETREAT

A number of essential factors are identified in the organizational development literature that contribute to a successful retreat, and we found these factors to be important to a professional group as well. First, the retreat should be initiated by the organization's top management (Dyer, 1977). Second, appropriate leaders should be selected to conduct the retreats (French and Bell, 1978). Third, activities should focus on group tasks rather than relationships (Huse, 1980). Fourth, members should recognize that retreats are part of an ongoing program for developing and maintaining organizational effectiveness, and are not a panacea. Fifth, each retreat should be designed to address the current needs of the organization, to set clear goals, and to create a climate that is conducive to success. Sixth, enlisting the participation and enthusiasm of those scheduled to attend a retreat is also essential. They should be involved in planning the retreat, in outlining the agenda, and in determining the goals (French and Bell, 1978). Finally, if more than one retreat is planned, each retreat should ideally build upon the momentum and successes of previous meetings.

Once it has been decided to hold a retreat, the first step is to establish clear goals. What is it in particular that the organization hopes to accomplish by means of the retreat? How will these goals be defined? Once these goals are attained, how will they be continued within the organization? In addition, certain methodological quetions need to be addressed. Who should come? When and for how long should the meeting take place? Where should it be held? How can everyone be encouraged to participate? What activities should be used?

The decision regarding who will attend a retreat should, of course, be determined by the goals of the particular retreat. The length will also depend on the goals, as well as on certain practical limitations. Staff commitment to take the time to hold a retreat is far more important than its actual length of time (Dyer, 1977). However, since a certain amount of settling-in time is required whenever a group meets, at least half a day seems to be a necessary minimum as a block of time.

In choosing a location for a retreat, an off-site location is preferable because it provides a setting where participants can give their full time and attention to problem solving free from the usual distractions, and where people can relax and enjoy themselves more freely. The setting need not be a great distance away. Retreats can be held quite close to the office, perhaps at an apartment clubhouse or at a staff member's private home. Activities should provide the means for achieving the objectives of the retreat. For example, included might be group discussions, individual and group goal-setting exercises, and movies as well as sports, meals, etc.

Finally, planning follow-up activities is crucial to ensure the success of retreats. According to Dyer (1977), "Unless the decisions made and actions planned are actually implemented, the excitement and enthusiasm generated is likely to be lost." Ideally, at least one person will be designated to follow-up on ideas generated at each retreat since a high level of perserverance is often needed to maintain the momentum for change.

THE CAPS EXPERIENCE

While the particular problems faced by CAPS may be unique, the authors feel that the process of individual growth and organizational enhancement brought about as a result of our staff retreats may be widely applicable.

As noted in Chapter III, CAPS was established in the summer of 1977 when the former Student Mental Health Service and Counseling Center were merged. This new multi-disciplinary organization sought to provide direct counseling, psychiatric services, outreach education, and consultation. The director recognized that a strong organization was essential in order to achieve the primary goal of delivering these services to students in the most effective manner possible. Thus, the director's organizational objectives were to gain maximum staff participation in planning and problem-solving, to provide a climate that would allow staff members to achieve personal and professional goals, and to foster a sense of high morale and job satisfaction.

One means by which the director sought to achieve these goals was the initiation of retreats. In planning retreats, the director hoped to provide an ongoing effort to facilitate the integration of professionals from different disciplines (Fulkerson, et al., 1980) and to minimize the possibility of burnout by professionals continually faced with intangible results and a seemingly endless flow of problems. Thus, a retreat also legitimizes the need for periodic rest and recuperation (Levinson, 1981).

In addition, disruptions caused by the rapid growth of the organization created obstacles to attaining organizational goals. This needed to be addressed. Greiner (1972) has defined predictable stages of growth and development encountered by most organizations. After one year of operation, CAPS had moved through the first two of these stages: creativity and direction and had entered the third, "a crisis of delegation." As noted in Chapter III, the increasing size of the staff and complexity of the organization required the director to devote more time to broader administrative issues. Therefore, coordinators were appointed to facilitate the functioning of five major areas at CAPS: clinical services; consultation; training; vocational planning, outreach and testing; and research and program evaluation. This new organizational transition required considerably more staff communication as it evoked new challenges and the need to clarify changing roles. The retreats were designed to meet the needs engendered by these changes in the organization.

The organization structure itself at CAPS had created obstacles to maintaining two key organizational objectives: active staff participation and high morale. Thompson (1967) defined the structure of an organization as "the internal differentiation and patterning of relationships within the organization." According to his definition, the predominant structure at CAPS would be "pooled interdependence" since therapists work independently and influence each other's work only slightly. The professional staff relies only minimally on each other to perform their daily tasks and work most of the day with students in their individual offices, resulting in little time being spent with colleagues. This separation is further compounded by differences in professional disciplines and experience, and a large proportion of part-time staff. Thus, a retreat seemed to be one effective means for bridging these gaps.

The retreat planners, then, were looking for ways to increase staff participation in organizational goal setting and planning. The planners were also attempting to facilitate the maintenance of high morale, improve task performance, strength group cohesion and enhance multidisciplinary cooperation. Easing the problem of delegation and preventing therapist burnout were also goals. The organization needed a method of intervention that would overcome the separation of colleagues caused by the organizational structure (i.e., one that would get the staff together and provide ample time to adequately address these issues in a favorable setting).

The director asked three staff members who were enthusiastic about the idea of a retreat and skilled in conducting seminars and structured groups to design and lead the early retreats. Through the process of solving problems together, more *esprit de corps* developed among the staff. On the other hand, the participants had enough healthy skepticism about the feasibility of what could be accomplished to counteract unrealistically high hopes.

The CAPS' retreats were held in a condominium clubhouse or a private home and were attended by all professional senior staff members and, at various times support staff (administrative and clerical) as well as those in training. The length of each retreat was determined by both the goals of the retreat and practical limitations. Consequently, they varied in length from two full days and an evening to one-half day. The CAPS staff took advantage of the natural break between regular academic terms to plan the summer retreats. Because the clinical workload is customarily lighter then, staff members were able to take more time away from the office. In contrast, the heavy service demands during the academic year made the need for a break in the work schedule all the more important, but more difficult to arrange. In planning the activities for the retreats, structured work activities were alternated with relaxed breaks. Humor was used to facilitate communication by playing silly music, wearing witty name tags, etc. (Barrow, et al, 1981). Participants relaxed by eating meals together, listening to music, and playing group sports. An attempt was made to involve the participants as whole persons, and not just as workers (French and Bell, 1978).

The steps outlined above were taken to develop group cohesion, provide rest and relaxation, and to create a setting for the "timely exchange of essential information, views, and decisions" (Levinson, 1981). What follows is a brief description of the particular objectives and achievements of each retreat.

The goals of the first retreat were: (1) to smooth out the problems around delegation experienced by the organization, (2) to identify organizational problems and goals, (3) to help individuals plan career goals, and (4) to integrate a new staff member. This retreat was attended by the eight senior staff members and lasted two days and an evening. At this first retreat, activities were designed to address the problems of delegation and to help the new staff member understand his role at CAPS. In addition, this retreat generated possible solutions for five major problems that had been identified. First, the staff recognized the untapped potential of several support staff and identified the importance of improving the quality of their work life. Second, the decision was made to offer career planning groups to students for the first time. Third, it was recommended that another psychology intern be added to the staff. Fourth, as a result of the individual goal-setting exercises, it was decided that individual schedules would be arranged to provide small blocks of time uninterrupted by seeing students so that staff members could pursue professional reading and writing. Fifth, all present identified the need to find continuing ways to reduce stress by reaffirming the importance of compensatory time. One person was designated to follow the outcome of each action planned.

The major emphases of the second retreat were to recognize staff achievements that had occurred since the first retreat and to promote a fruitful exchange of ideas between the senior staff and those in training who attended this one day retreat. Another goal was to help the professionals in training focus on setting individual professional objectives. The second retreat identified the need for a reduction of work-related stress and more effective time management. A psychology intern volunteered to lead a time management seminar following the retreat. An afternoon "brainstorming" session generated ideas such as investigating the purchase of video equipment, developing a manual for new staff, and exploring the possibility of acquiring a work/study student to help with office and research tasks. Volunteers agreed to take responsibility to oversee the implementation of each of these tasks.

The third retreat focused on training. In addition to expanding the goals of the earlier retreats, to recognize achievements and to have fun, the staff members focused on preparing for the addition to the CAPS staff of several new professionals in training. The format included a discussion of potential problems associated with the rapidly enlarging staff and the acknowledgment that adjustments would be required by everyone. This retreat lasted for one full day, with the senior staff attending a morning session, joined by the support staff for lunch and the afternoon session. In addition, the following accomplishments that were generated as goals at past retreats were celebrated: (1) the inclusion of the support staff at the retreat, (2) the completion of a very successful time management seminar for the professional staff, (3) the approval of funding for a third psychology intern, (4) the completion of an assertiveness training seminar for support staff, (5) the acquisition of two work/study students, and (6) the completion of a preliminary manual of CAPS policies and procedures.

Inherent organizational resistance became evident as the time to plan the fourth retreat approached. The director and two of the three previous leaders informally expressed feelings that everyone might be too busy to attend a retreat and that perhaps it should be postponed indefinitely. The leaders questioned their own commitment to conducting another retreat. Others questioned the efficacy of holding a retreat if there were no urgent problems currently to address. Other staff members felt, however, that the retreats had helped to keep their investment in CAPS alive and that they were essential for the prevention of future problems. They also pointed out that this retreat would not entail as much planning, since the norms and general format for the retreats already had been established. With continued interest evident, the fourth retreat was planned, and the leadership was rotated to two staff members expressing continued enthusiasm. The previous leaders met with the new leaders to plan this retreat in order to ensure continuity. As a result of this transition period, the overall staff commitment to holding retreats has strengthened.

At the fourth retreat, ideas were generated to improve the functioning of the weekly multidisciplinary team case conferences. A special emphasis was placed on incorporating the valuable perspectives offered by those in training who were by then familiar with the organization. This retreat was held for only half a day as a result of the particularly intense time demands for direct service. All staff members, including support staff, were present for a leisurely lunch. The professional staff attended the afternoon session. The results of an anonymous questionnaire for improving team functioning were used in a brainstorming session regarding constructive changes that might be made.

Conclusion

At CAPS, retreats have contributed significantly to the ongoing process of organizational development by an emphasis on setting, achieving, and maintaining organizational objectives. The retreats have helped in attaining and continuing high levels of staff participation in problem-solving, enhancing individual job satisfaction, group cohesion, and preventing burnout. They have also served as vehicles to allow staff members to take stock of their own performance, to celebrate their accomplishments, and to make sure that staff members know that their contributions have been important to the organization. Retreats have helped to counteract the strong tendency of individuals and organizations to solve problems as they arise rather than to do anticipatory planning for them. In other words, a retreat can help an organization manage change positively rather than just react to it. The retreats have helped to minimize the isolating aspects of the organization's structure and the possibility of burnout common to people working in the helping professions.

As a result of the success of the four retreats described here, the CAPS staff now has retreats on a regular basis. We recommend retreats to improve the quality of work life for the staff and to facilitate an ongoing renewal process in a university counseling and psychological services organization and thus as a significant way to ultimately provide better services for students. The staff at CAPS has found that to retreat is, indeed, to advance.

REFERENCES

1. Barrow, J., Fulkerson, K., and Moore, C.: The Use of Humor as a Teaching Tool in Outreach Educational Interventions. Read before the Annual Convention of the American College Personnel Association, Cincinnati, March, 1981.
2. Dyer, G.: *Team Building: Issues and Alternatives.* Reading, Addison-Wesley Publishing Company, Inc., 1977.
3. French, L., and Bell, H.: *Organizational Development.* Englewood Cliffs, N.J., Prentice-Hall, Inc., 1978.
4. Fulkerson, C. F., Newton, F. B., and Roy, E. T.: Perspectives for the 80's in a College Counseling Center: A '3-D' Approach — Diversity of Staff, Developmental Themes, Delivery through Groups. Read before the Annual Meeting of the American College Health Association, San Diego, 1980.

5. Greiner, L.: Evolution and revolution as organizations grow. *Harvard Business Review, 50*:37-46, 1972.

6. Huse, E. F.: *Organization Development and Change,* 2nd ed. St. Paul, West Publishing Company, 1980.

7. Levinson, H.: When executives burnout. *Harvard Business Review, 59*:73-81, 1981.

8. Thompson, J. D.: *Organizations in Action.* New York, McGraw Hill Publishing Company, 1967.

AUTHOR INDEX

SUBJECT INDEX

A

Academic performance
effect of depression on, 52
Accountability, 50
Administrators, university
commitment to services of, 35
responsibility for students of, 63, 68
Adolescence, late,
definition of, 33
Age
counseling needs and, 25-26
service use and, 6, 7, 14-15
Alcohol, use of
reported problems with, 18, 19, 26
service sought regarding, 11
American College Health Association
Recommended Practices of the (1964),
65
Anxiety,
Treatment sought regarding, 11
Assertiveness
reported need for, 19, 21
Assessment (*see* Intake screening)

B

Beck Depression Inventory, 51
Birth control, reported need for, 19
Burnout, 94, 95, 98

C

CAPS (*see* Counseling and psychological
services)
Career choice, 18, 21 (*see also* Vocational
identity)
Career couple, two, problems as a, 24
Change, management of, 95, 102

Clients (*see also* Patients) student, 3-17
Colleges in the United States, 1
population of, 4
Combined services (*see* Merged services)
Conflicts, personal, needs regarding,
19
Confidentiality, 40, 63, 64, 67-70, 76
Consultation
mental health professionals and, 64, 67-
68
University administrators and, 63, 67
Counseling and mental health centers
comparison between, 4-5
demand for, 50
(*see also* Merged services)
Counseling and Psychological Services
Duke University, 31-48
development of, 44-46
mandate for, 38

D

Death of parent and service use, 12
Decision-making
reported problem with, 21
Depression, assessment of, 51
males *vs.* females, and the, 52
Developmental tasks of students, 32-34
Diagnoses, 13-15, table 13-14
Divorce of parents and service use, 12
Dropping out, 83-85
Drug problems
reported, 18, 19, 26
service sought for, 11
Duke University
The Committee on Counseling Services,
35